Martial Arts™

the

judo

handbook

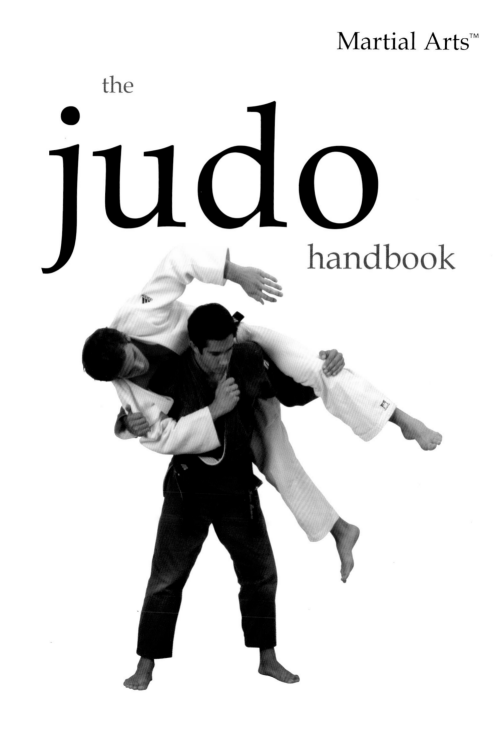

Martial Arts™

the

judo

handbook

Roy Inman

ROSEN
PUBLISHING®

New York

This North American edition published in 2008 by:

The Rosen Publishing Group, Inc.

29 East 21st Street

New York, NY 10010

North American edition, this format, printed in 2008
by The Rosen Publishing Group, Inc.

GV1114.I56 2008

796.815'2—dc22

2007037742

Manufactured in China

Creative Director: Sarah King

Project editor: Jean Coppendale

Designer: Debbie Fisher

Photographer: Colin Bowling/Paul Forrester

Library of Congress Cataloging-in-Publication

Inman, Roy.

The judo handbook / Roy Inman. — North American ed.

    p. cm. — (Martial arts)

Includes bibliographical references and index.

ISBN-13: 978-1-4042-1393-7 (library binding)

1. Judo. I. Title.

contents

history, origins, and philosophy of judo

Judo means different things to different people; what it means to you depends very much on your reasons for taking part in judo and what you expect to gain from it. To some, judo is a fun activity, a competitive sport, a way of socializing or a fitness regime. To others, it is a means of self-defense, a way of challenging aggression or a form of combat. To experts, like Jigoro Kano himself, judo is a way of life.

How it all began

Kodokan Judo originated in Japan and owes its existence to Jigoro Kano, who was born in Mikage, Hyogo district, in western Japan on October 28, 1860. It has been said that Kano was physically weak in his early years and that he was the target of local bullies. This gave Kano an incentive to learn how to defend himself, and ultimately resulted in the development of judo.

At the age of 17 Kano moved to Tokyo, where he was introduced to Ryuji Katagiri, a jujitsu teacher. However, Ryuji Katagiri believed Kano was too young for serious training and taught him only a few basic exercises. Not to be put off, Kano found the dojo (school) of HachinosUke Fukuda, who was a master in the Tenji-shinyo school of jujitsu. Master Fukuda had a different approach to Jigoro's former teacher, and encouraged him to practice randori (free-style fighting) rather than the kata (formal exercises) preferred by Katagiri.

A year after he began his jujitsu training, Kano started attending the Tokyo Imperial University. In 1879, just one year after he had begun training at the Tenjin-shinyo school of jujitsu, his master died. Kano's next instructor was Masatomo Iso, whose dojo was renowned for its excellence in kata.

Jigoro Kano absorbed himself in jujitsu and practiced whenever he could for the next two years. His sensei (coach) rewarded his dedication by making him an assistant and in 1881, at the age of 21, as well as graduating from Tokyo Imperial University, Kano became a master in Tenjin-shinyo-ryu jujitsu. When his master, Masatomo Iso, became ill, Kano moved on in search of greater knowledge. He joined the Kito school of jujitsu and trained under master Tsunetoshi Iikubo, who was highly skilled at teaching nage waza (throwing techniques) and opted for more free-style fighting.

The birth of judo

While Kano was at Tenjin-shinyo, his interest in developing a way to defend himself was stimulated still further. At the school he met Kenkichi Fukushima and, weighing about 100 lbs (55 kg) less than Kenkichi Fukushima, Kano invariably lost any match against him. This frustrated Kano so much that he studied and trained even harder. He developed his own techniques and eventually defeated Kenkichi Fukushima with what he later called a kata guruma (shoulder wheel, see page 54).

Initially, Kano had set about improving jujitsu: it had not been his intention to develop a

completely new system of self-defense. However, he had discovered weaknesses in jujitsu and felt he could develop his own ideas as a martial art, not only as a type of physical education but also, more importantly, as a discipline of the mind and spirit.

The transition from jujitsu to judo was by no means immediate. In February 1882, with nine of his private students from the Kito school, Kano started his own dojo in the Eishoji Buddhist temple, based in the Tokyo district of Shitaya Inaricho. He named his new judo club the Kodokan. *Ko* means to teach, study and learn, *do* refers to the "way" or path, and *kan* means hall, so *kodokan* literally means "the place to learn the way of judo."

Initially, in his Kodokan Kano Juku (academy) the training was mainly in jujitsu. The Kito-ryu master, Iikubo, regularly visited and instructed Kano's students. It is not known exactly when the jujitsu taught at Eishoji temple became judo, but it is possible that it coincided with the first time Kano defeated his master Iikubo in randori.

A new way of thinking

To distinguish his new martial art and sport from jujitsu, Kano called his system judo. The literal translation of *judo* means "way of non-resistance," which is often simplified to "gentle way." In Kano's system, Ukemi waza (breakfall techniques, see page 16) were designed to add an element of safety, which in turn allowed greater progression in randori. Kano removed the elements of jujitsu that he considered to be dangerous, eliminating most kicks, punches and strikes. Traditionally, most jujitsu schools only practiced kata (prearranged patterns of techniques) with co-operative partners. Now, Kano taught kata for skill acquisition but also promoted randori, which offered a more realistic experience of unarmed combat.

However, the most significant difference between jujitsu and judo lies with the do (way): to Kano, judo is a way of life. He developed what is known as kuzushi, the breaking of balance (which is what enabled him to defeat master Iikubo). The principle is that a small amount of force is used to change an opponent's posture and draw him or her off balance, thereby allowing the opponent to be thrown. Kano maintained that this is possible regardless of whether the opponent is heavier. Put another way, Kano believed that one can maximize one's power by using one's brain. For example, when an opponent pushes, one should pull, and when an opponent pulls, one should push. As a result, control is gained over an opponent, irrespective of his or her size.

The growth of the school

Kano was a disciplinarian and tough on his students, but he was also a generous person. Not wanting his poorer students to be at a disadvantage, he provided them with freshly laundered clothes to practice in.

In 1886, rivalry from local jujitsu schools grew. This culminated in a grand tournament,

overseen by the Chief of Tokyo Metropolitan Police, between Kano's Kodokan and the Totsuka jujitsu school. Kano could not afford for his team to lose, as defeat would diminish his credibility. However, he had nothing to worry about as his school won a decisive victory. Fifteen handpicked students from each school battled for supremacy. Kano's students won all but two contests and those two were declared a draw. As a result, the Japanese government granted the Kodokan school official recognition.

The school changed addresses several times in the years that followed, as interest in the new sport grew and the need for larger premises arose. After just five years the Kodokan school had over 1,500 members.

In 1889, hoping to make judo more popular throughout Japan, Kano turned his attention to sharing his knowledge with the rest of the world. The Kodokan school established the first gokyo (Gokyo waza are the five sets, currently comprising forty throws, of Kodokan judo) in 1895, which consisted of forty-two throws.

In 1909, the Kodokan became an official foundation, with a judo teachers' training department established in 1911. Kano travelled widely telling people about his newly developed sport and intended to create an international judo federation. The Dan Grade Holders' Association was developed in 1922, followed in 1932 by the Judo Medical Research Society. Prior to the First World War, dojos were established in Britain, France, Canada, the United States, Russia, China and Korea.

Kano's lasting influence

Shortly after graduating from Tokyo Imperial University, Kano began teaching at Gakushuin school, and by the age of twenty-five, he was appointed headmaster. Prior to Kano's appointment, Gakushuin was only attended by children from the imperial family and upper-class families. However, Kano refused to believe that academic potential was determined by status. He transformed Gakushuin into a boarding school, where he instilled discipline. Jigoro Kano's influence as headmaster of both Gakushuin and, in later years, the Tokyo Teacher-Training School (now the Tokyo University of Education) shaped modern education in Japan.

In 1909, Jigoro Kano became the first ever Japanese representative of the International Olympic Committee. Although there is no doubt that Kano's first love was judo, he was interested in all sports. He founded the Japan Athletic Association (JAA) in 1911, becoming the first president. He attended the 5th Olympiad in Stockholm in 1912, which was the first time Japan had participated.

Although he was not against weight divisions in judo, Kano strongly believed that a small man is able to throw a large man with ease. However, weight categories were introduced. There were four categories at the Tokyo Olympics in 1964: lightweight, under 139 lbs (63 kg); middleweight, under 176 lbs (80 kg); heavyweight, under 205 lbs (93 kg) and the open weight.

Kano continued to teach and practice judo into the later years of his life—albeit with a more educational and spiritual focus, as he no longer participated in randori himself.

Despite his efforts to promote Tokyo as a suitable host of the 1940 Olympic Games, the Second World War intervened and Tokyo had to wait until 1964 to become the host nation. Sadly, despite all his efforts, Kano did not live to see his beloved judo become an Olympic sport. He died from pneumonia on May 4, 1938, at age seventy-eight.

However, his legacy continues: in 1952 Kano's dream of an International Judo Federation (IJF) became a reality; in 1956 Tokyo held the first world judo championships. Then in 1964, when Japan hosted the olympics, judo was included as an event for the first time, attracting seventy-four participants from twenty-seven different countries. There were just four weight categories and no women's competition. The Japanese dominated, but perhaps as a symbol of the growth of judo throughout the West, Anton Geesink of Holland beat Akio Kaminaga from Japan in the final in the open-weight category.

Women's judo (joshi judo)

It was not until 1923 that a women's section was formally established at the Kaiunzaka dojo. Formal tuition for women began in 1926 adopting a system that has become the basis of the present-day Kodokan women's section. Initially the women trained in kata and performed light randori; they were not permitted to engage in full-out randori as the men did.

Then in 1980, the first-ever world judo championships open to women took place. Competitors entered from twenty-seven different countries. In the 1988 Seoul Olympic Games, women's judo was a demonstration event. Following its success, women's judo was eventually recognized by the International Olympic Committee and in 1992 in Barcelona, the 25th Olympiad, women's judo became an event in its own right.

chapter 1:

fundamental aspects of Kodokan Judo

Judo is a Japanese martial art that is practiced around the world by millions of people of all ages, races, and physical abilities. It is equally suitable for men and women as it relies on technique rather than pure physical strength.

Dojo and tatame

A dojo merely refers to the place were judo is practiced. In this dojo is the tatame (mat). Throughout the years the design of the tatame has advanced to enhance safety without inhibiting speed of movement.

Dojo training areas can vary dramatically in size from 20 x 20 ft (6 m x 6 m) to 390 sq ft (100 m^2). A competition area is a minimum of 46 x 46 ft (14 m x 14 m) and a maximum of 53 x 53 ft (16 m x 16 m). This includes the red area (the danger area) and the safety area around the outside. Therefore, the actual contest area itself must be between 26 x 26 ft (8 m x 8 m) and 33 x 33 ft (10 m x 10 m).

Judoka

A judoka is someone who participates in the martial art of judo. "Uke" is the term used for the person being thrown. "Tori" is the term used for the person executing the technique.

Judogi

Judogi represents clothing, that is the trousers, jacket, and belt. Judo is practiced wearing a judogi based on the theory that, if attacked, one's opponent is likely to be clothed. However, everyday clothes would not be able to withstand frequent training sessions, so a strengthened, double-weave jacket was designed.

Traditionally a judoka wore a jacket with short sleeves and short trousers, leaving most of the arms and legs exposed. However, in 1907, Kano redesigned the judogi to provide more protection. He lengthened the sleeves and trouser legs and also shortened the jacket. This is the type of judogi that judokas wear today.

The judogi is a fundamental part of judo. So much so, that there are now stringent regulations on the length and width of the sleeves and trouser legs, and also on the amount of crossover on the jacket. This is because competitive judokas used to take the rules to the limits and their kits became shorter and shorter and so more difficult to grip. From a sporting perspective, judokas utilize the style of the judogi to optimize throwing, holding, strangling, and armlock techniques

When on the tatame a judoka has bare feet. It is part of judo etiquette not to walk on the tatame with shoes but to wear some form of footwear off the mat. Traditionally, zori are worn to and from the place of practice. Zori are similar to flip-flops and used to be made from straw.

Etiquette

For reasons of hygiene, safety, self-discipline, respect and good sportsmanship, judokas are required to wear clean judogi, to ensure good personal hygiene, to have short nails, to tie back long hair and to have no footwear on the tatame but to wear some form of zori off the mat. There should be no unnecessary talking within the

A demonstration of a zarei (kneeling bow). This is usually performed at the beginning and end of a training session or newaza randori (ground work free practice).

as a group to the highest grade at the beginning and end of a practice. A judoka always bows to an opponent before and after practice and the same etiquette applies at a judo competition. The philosophy behind this is to show respect for your place of training, your sensei, your opponents and your sport.

practice environment. Respect is a very important element in judo; a judoka should respect his sensei and other judokas. Rei is an expression of respect and consideration signified by a standing (ritsurei) or kneeling bow (zarei). A judoka performs a ritsurei when entering and leaving the dojo. A zarei is made

The judka (pupils) bow to their sensei (teacher or coach).

A demonstration of a ritsurei (standing bow). This is normal etiquette at the beginning and end of a contest or training bout.

Ukemi waza (breakfall techniques)

Ukemi or breakfall techniques are moves that have been designed specifically to protect the body when being thrown. One of the major training aids for judo, these techniques are used by beginners and Olympians alike. They enable judokas to practice throwing each other on the tatame, and the action of the breakfall avoids injury. The secret of any breakfall technique is being able to relax your body as you are being thrown. This comes with practice!

Usually, when practicing breakfall techniques for the first time, they are performed close to the ground to lessen the impact and to allow the judoka to gain confidence and correct the technique before advancing to an upright position. It is important to learn breakfalls on both sides, as you cannot choose which way an opponent will throw you. In order to learn these techniques correctly, beginners should seek the advice and guidance of a qualified judo sensei.

Backward breakfall

Stage 1

The judoka lies flat on his back, with knees bent and his back flat against the tatame. He places the arms across the body and then slaps the mat, making sure to keep the arms straight by his side as he does so.

Stage 2

The judoka then crouches down with his arms straight by his sides (the tips of the fingers can be used to maintain balance).

Stage 3

He then rolls backward and, as his back touches the mat, he slaps the mat with his hands.

Side breakfalls

This is a single-arm breakfall.

Stages 1 and 2

From a squat position, the judoka pushes one leg across in front of the other and rolls onto his side.

Stage 3

On contact with the mat, the judoka slaps it with this free arm. Once confidence is built, this can be performed from a standing position.

A useful training drill for the side breakfall can be done in pairs. Uke is on his hands and knees in a press-up position, Tori reaches under Uke's body, takes the far arm and pulls it through, maintaining the grip in order to support Uke. As Uke spins round he slaps the mat in a side breakfall. NB: A major part of this training relies on Tori's support.

Stage 2

Stage 1

Note the body stance and hand preparation before the performance of the breakfall.

Stage 3

Landing position.

Forward rolling breakfall

Here, the action is similar to a forward roll although, unlike gymnastics, it is important that the head does not touch the mat for safety reasons. This type of roll is executed to the judoka's diagonal, and it is the shoulder, not the head, that makes contact with the tatame.

Stage 1

Stage 1

Starting in an upright position, the judoka places one foot forward (it is usually best to learn this on your dominant side first and progress to the other side) and reaches forward with the arm on the same side.

Stage 2

The judoka turns his hand under, toward his own body. (It is advisable to take the advice of a judo sensei to ensure that this is done correctly.) The other hand can be used to assist balance.

Stage 3

The judoka pushes off with the back leg, his shoulder makes contact with the mat and he slaps the mat.

Stage 2

Stage 3

Flat forward breakfall

Another breakfall that is used is when the judoka falls forward with a relaxed body. The head is turned sideways to prevent landing on the face. The judoka lands on his forearms and palms, thus preventing injury and absorbing the impact of the fall. The toes are tucked under, which protects the knees and torso by raising them off the mat.

Grips

A standard right-handed grip is where Tori holds Uke's right lapel midway above belt level, with his right hand, thumb uppermost, while the left hand holds the sleeve below Uke's elbow. For a right-handed technique Tori turns his body in an counterclockwise direction.

Right-handed grip

Left-handed grip

For left-handers, or those who want to train on both sides, the left hand holds the lapel, again with the thumb uppermost, and the right hand holds the sleeve. A left-handed technique is generally done in a clockwise direction, although it is possible to hold right and throw left and vice versa. From the standard grip a judoka can adopt a variety of grips, bearing in mind that penalties are given for nonstandard grips, where a technique is not executed immediately. For example, if a judoka holds the trouser leg, belt or same side of the jacket with both hands and does not attack straight away, a penalty will ensue.

Traditional judo training methods

Judo starts with opponents taking hold of each other, so the distance between each judoka is usually arm's length. To be successful, a judo throw requires the space between judokas to be closed down, which is achieved by stepping toward each other, pulling and bypassing any blocks. The movement can be made in a one-step, two-step or three-step pattern, achieving body contact before lifting, and/or rotating and/or sweeping the opponent causing him or her to lose balance.

One-step pattern

With a one-step pattern the throwing position is achieved in one movement, which means that the throwing leg is also the stepping leg.

Two-step pattern

This requires two steps to achieve the throwing position. The first step establishes positioning and the second step is also the throw.

Three-step pattern

These are techniques that require three steps on entry into the technique. The first step is usually a step forward. The second step repositions the body and the third step completes the throw.

It is important to practice the various aspects of traditional judo training. This is best achieved with a partner so that you can practice gripping, blocking and throwing each other in turns. To start with uchikomi, or skill repetition work, involves positioning the body with various step patterns. Then kazushi is the technique of breaking an opponent's balance and nage komi is the completion of the throw.

Competitive scoring system

The objective of winning in the sport of judo is to throw an opponent with impetus onto the back.

Ippon

Ippon actually means "one whole point," but is given the value of ten points and an outright win. Ippon is signified by the referee raising his arm straight up in the air and simultaneously shouting "ippon." Ippon is achieved by throwing an opponent flat on his or her back with impetus; controlling him for twenty-five seconds in a recognized judo hold-down; obtaining a submission from a strangle or armlock; or if the referee sees fit to intervene. There is another way of achieving ippon: if a judoka gains two waza ari scores (see below) they combine to equal ippon.

Waza ari

Waza ari is a seven-point score and is signified by the referee stretching out his arm at a 90-degree angle and calling "waza ari." Waza ari is given for something that is not quite an ippon. It is achieved when an opponent is thrown largely onto his or her back and/or without some of the impetus required for an ippon or by controlling an opponent on his or her back for twenty to twenty-four seconds.

Yuko

A yuko is a five-point score. A referee signals a yuko by announcing "yuko" and holding out a straight arm at a 45-degree angle from his leg. Yuko is achieved by throwing an opponent onto his or her side, but without speed and/or force, or by holding an opponent for between fifteen and nineteen seconds. Yukos are not accumulative, so regardless of the number of yukos scored, a waza ari is always worth more.

Koka

A koka is a minor score, worth three points, shown by the referee bending his arm by his shoulder with an open hand and the palm facing forward. A koka is achieved when an opponent lands on his or her buttocks, thigh, or shoulder or when osaekomi (a hold-down) is held for ten to fourteen seconds. As with yukos, kokas are not accumulative, so no amount of kokas are deemed equal to or greater than a yuko.

Scores are also awarded for shidos (penalties), which range from slight infringements to disqualifiable offenses. If a competitor receives a shido, this becomes an equivalent positive score for the opponent.

If the time has elapsed and no outright win has been achieved, the winner of the contest is the competitor who has attained the highest of the above scores. However, if there are no scores or the scores are drawn, the competitors move into the "golden score."

Golden score

If, at the end of the allocated time scores are equal, time is added (usually the duration of the contest) for a sudden-death round, where the first score wins, just like a golden goal in football.

If, within extra time, there is still no score, the two corner judges and the center referee are required to make a decision by raising flags that correspond to the color of the competitor's suit or belt, in support of the judoka they consider to be the closest to throwing or the one who made the most attacks. The winner is the one with the majority of flags in his favor.

Officials

Generally there is a center referee and two corner judges assisted by timekeepers and contest recorders at each contest area. The time of a contest is usually five minutes for men and women and a shorter time, usually three minutes, dependent on age, for juniors.

A gold medallist in a tournament would average six to seven contests within the day depending on the fighting system used—a pool system or straight knockout (see page 27).

Achieving judo skills and grading within judo

The traditional way of progressing in judo is to train in three activities. The first is skill training and studying the intricacies of where and how to move the various parts of the body. The second is randori, free practice, where skills and techniques are tested out in relatively realistic situations. Thirdly, there is proactive fighting in competition (called shiai) where mistakes are costly to the outcome.

Not all judokas enter Olympic trials or major tournaments. Normally their first experience of competition is at a judo grading. The judo grade system has been in existence since judo first began. Normally starting with a light, white belt the belts grow darker as you progress through the grades and denote the skill, knowledge and experience of the wearer. The colors might vary slightly, but a normal system is: beginner belt white, then yellow, orange, green, blue and brown. These are called kyu, or beginner, grades. After brown comes the coveted black belt, the dan, or advanced grade.

A normal exam requirement would be for the judoka to fight opponents of the same or similar grades and have knowledge of and be able to demonstrate specific judo techniques. This applies up to 5th dan black belt, obviously with the requirements becoming progressively more difficult. Above that grade, 6th dan changes to a red-and-white belt, eventually reaching 9th and 10th dan, when it becomes red. Normally grades after 5th dan are awarded for time, knowledge, experience and service in the sport.

level	grade	
Beginner		white belt
5th kyu		yellow belt
4th kyu		orange belt
3rd kyu		green belt
2nd kyu		blue belt
1st kyu		brown belt
1st – 5th dan		black belt
6th – 8th dan		red-and-white belt
9th – 10th dan		red belt

Competition judo

If you are a competitor entering a judo event you will fight in your weight category. Currently in the Olympic games there are seven different weight categories for men and women.

Men:	Women:
under (132 lb) 60 kg	under (105 lb) 48 kg
under (145 lb) 66 kg	under (114 lb) 52 kg
under (160 lb) 73 kg	under (125 lb) 57 kg
under (178 lb) 81 kg	under (138 lb) 63 kg
under (209 lb) 95 kg	under (154 lb) 70 kg
under (220 lb) 100 kg	under (39 lb) 78 kg
over (50 lb) 100 kg	over (39 lb) 78kg

Contests are run using either a pool system, whereby competitors are put into groups and the top two from each group go through into the next round, or a straight knockout system, where competitors only progress to the next round if they win each fight. This includes a repecharge system, where competitors who lose to the semifinalists battle it out for the bronze medal positions.

Kata

Traditionally handed down through the centuries, kata training is a style of judo training that involves specific movements with no variation. They contain idealized, set patterns of techniques that depict specific judo principles.

The set patterns are not demonstrated in this book, as it focuses on a more competitive style of judo.

There are seven formal katas in judo:

Nage no kata: a set of Kodokan Judo formal throwing techniques.

Katame no kata: a set of Kodokan Judo formal groundwork techniques.

Go no sen no kata: a set of Kodokan Judo formal counter-throwing (reactive) techniques.

Koshiki no kata: a set of Kodokan Judo formal techniques. These are the classic forms that were inherited from the Kito-ryu jujitsu school.

Kime no kata: a set of Kodokan Judo formal techniques designed to teach the fundamentals of defense against an attack. These attacks are throwing, grappling and striking techniques. Sometimes known as the self-defense form.

Itsutsu no kata: a set of five Kodokan Judo formal techniques used to express principles of attack and defense.

Ju no kata: a set of Kodokan Judo formal techniques formulated to allow judokas to practice judo moves without a judogi or a judo dojo. They are forms of flexibility and gentleness.

Randori

Randori is free practice or free sparring without the presence of referees, allowing the judoka to practice in a relatively realistic (to competition) situation. All the techniques in this book can be used in randori and competition.

chapter 2:

Nage waza (throwing techniques)

Nage waza is the Japanese term for throwing techniques. To avoid confusion, all throws in this book are demonstrated to the right. If you are left-handed, simply reverse the hand positions and direction of the turn (if applicable) shown. In fact, it is useful to practice the techniques on both sides as this helps to prevent any muscular imbalance and also serves to confuse one's opponent. For easy understanding of the techniques in this book, Tori is always wearing blue and Uke is wearing white.

Kazushi

It is important to realize that judo is not all about brute strength. An important lesson in judo is that of kazushi, the action of breaking an opponent's balance in preparation for the throw. Initially a judoka develops a feel for an opponent's weaknesses. This is done by Tori moving around the mat pushing and pulling Uke until there is a state of imbalance. Tori must capitalize on this imbalance and know when to attack and in which direction. This is most effectively achieved by using an opponent's resistance to a push or a pull, and throwing in the direction of that resistance.

The techniques in this section are listed in alphabetical order. To assist you in using the book and in locating certain types of technique, however, the throws have been categorized on the following pages into foot or leg techniques, hip techniques, hand techniques and sacrifice techniques.

Ashi waza (foot or leg techniques)

Koshi waza (hip techniques)

Te waza (hand techniques)

Sutemi waza (sacrifice techniques)

Ashi dori (leg grab)

1. Shows the single-hand lapel grip. Leaving the other hand free to execute the technique.

2. Demonstrates the hand placement on the outside of the knee.

Grip: Tori can have either a sleeve and lapel grip, removing the sleeve grip on entry, or just taking the one lapel.

Entry and execution: Tori uses the lapel grip and comes directly in for the attack, or has a sleeve and lapel grip and lets go of the sleeve grip on entry. Uke has his weight on the back leg and so is caught off guard. Tori bends her knees to lower her stance, still maintaining the lapel grip, reaches for Uke's far leg and either grips the trousers or cups the leg and drives her weight forward, taking Uke to the ground, pushing back and down with the lapel grip. There is a variety of leg grabs: for example, Tori can grip the lapel and leg on the same side of Uke, or on opposite sides, on the inside or outside of the leg.

Opportunity for attack: This technique is usually used when Uke has his weight on the back leg.

Related techniques: Morote gari (see page 66) or te otoshi (see page 112).

3. Demonstrates the hand control required to ensure that Uke lands on his back.

Ashi guruma (leg wheel)

Grip: The most effective grip for this technique is a high lapel grip, as it maximizes head control. However, a mid-lapel grip can also be used, accompanied by a low grip on the sleeve.

Entry and execution: Ashi guruma, as its name suggests, is a leg throw. Great timing and precision are essential to the success of this technique. Tori takes a lapel and sleeve grip. From an off-center stance Tori pivots on the ball of his left foot and swings his right leg across in front of Uke. Tori's calf should make contact with Uke's shin just below the knee, and the toe should be pointed. The leg is used as a block (it does not sweep). Tori rotates his body, pulling the sleeve in a circular movement and pushing round with the collar grip.

2. Emphasizes the head control required and the placement of the blocking leg.

1. Shows head control using the high collar grip with a low sleeve grip.

Opportunity for attack: This technique is usually used by taller judoka as the length of leg and body are an added asset to the throw. Ashi guruma works best when Uke is upright and standing slightly off center. Breaking an opponent's balance is difficult to do if he or she is a static entity, therefore this throw is facilitated if Uke moves round to Tori's left side. Tori may be able to influence Uke's movement by pulling round to make Uke step.

Related technique: Oguruma (see page 74).

Possible combinations and counter-techniques: Ashi guruma into tani otoshi (see page 173); Ashi guruma countered by te guruma (see page 194).

3. Demonstrates the rotation required to complete this technique.

Deashi barai/harai (advancing foot sweep)

Grip: Styles can be various: lapel and sleeve, two lapels or two sleeves. The most common grip pattern is mid-lapel and low sleeve.

Entry and execution: This technique is also sometimes known as deashi harai. Uke's movement is a major contributing factor to the success of this

1. Shows the mid-lapel grip and Uke's advanced left foot.

technique. As Uke steps forward, before his weight is placed on the advancing foot, Tori sweeps the outside of Uke's foot sideways, using the sole of the right foot. The power from the sweep is initiated from the hip. Tori then makes a circling, driving action with both hands to Uke's corner. If the technique is performed with precision timing, Uke should almost float up into the air with ease.

2. Demonstrates the foot placement required. Note the positioning of the sole of Tori's foot.

3. Maintaining the control with the lapel grip and the seeping action required.

Opportunity for attack: This technique is usually used against an opponent with an upright posture, and timing is essential to its success. The advancing foot sweep can be attempted if an opponent's arms feel strong or appear difficult to get past.

Related technique: Okuriashi barai/harai (see page 76).

Possible combinations and counter-techniques: Deashi barai into tomoe nage (see page 174); Deashi barai countered by kouchi gari (page 196).

Hane goshi (hip spring)

Grip: A high lapel or over the shoulder and low sleeve grip. The main objective of this high grip is to aim for chest contact.

Entry and execution: Tori uses a two-step entry, stepping in with the right leg, and swinging the left leg behind to become the support leg. Tori does not quite make a full turn

1. Shows the high over the shoulder and low sleeve grip. Note the space required between Tori and Uke.

2. Demonstrates the positioning of the leg and close body contact.

with his body, so he allows enough space to lift the right leg and prop it, in a bent position, against Uke's right leg, so that it acts as a platform. Tori pulls Uke's sleeve round in a semicircular action and rotates the upper body. The spring element of the technique refers to the straightening of the support leg and pushing of the bent platform leg.

Hane goshi is sometimes mistaken for uchimata (see page 122). However, if done correctly, Tori uses the leg as a prop and pushes Uke's leg in a sideways direction rather than swinging the leg backward as in uchimata.

3. Demonstrates the lifting action of Tori's leg.

Opportunity for attack: This throw can be used when Uke is in a slightly bent posture, with Uke standing still or moving backward, used as a catch-up movement.

Related technique: Hane makikomi (see page 40).

4. Shows the rotation of the shoulders required.

Hane makikomi
(springing wrap-around throw)

Grip: Initially a high lapel and low sleeve grip is established. However, to complete this technique the lapel grip is removed and wound round in a circular motion above Uke's right arm.

Entry and execution: Tori steps in using a standard right-handed grip. As with hane goshi, the right foot is followed by the left, which becomes the supporting leg and the right leg is used as a prop. The lapel grip is then removed.

1. Shows the low sleeve and the first attack position of the free arm.

2. Demonstrates the leg and body position required with the start of the action.

It is the change of grip that transforms what would be hane goshi into hane makikomi: greater body contact is achieved and a winding action is adopted to complete the throw. The technique is completed with a lifting action from the propping leg and a winding action of the body to the ground.

Opportunity for attack: This technique works well when Uke is preventing Tori from gaining a right-handed lapel grip and/or is controlling the left sleeve.

Related techniques: Harai makikomi (see page 44); osoto makikomi (see page 84); soto makikomi (see page 98); uchimata makikomi (see page 124); hane goshi (see page 38).

3. Shows the lifting action of the legs and the rotation required to complete the technique.

Harai goshi (sweeping hip)

Grip: A high or over-the-shoulder grip around the back of Uke's neck, and low sleeve grip are used. The high grip is used to gain control of the head and to establish chest contact.

Entry and execution: A two-step entry is adopted, with the right foot initiating the entry and the left foot swinging behind to become the support leg. The right leg is then brought back on to the front of Uke's thigh in a sweeping action. Execution of this technique is most effective if Tori's head and sweeping leg remain parallel. A breaking of Uke's balance to Uke's right front corner makes the throw most effective.

1. Shows the high over the shoulder and low sleeve grip.

Tori must be aware that if he is not committed, harai goshi can be susceptible to counters such as tani otoshi, ura nage and ushiro goshi. Therefore it is necessary for Tori to gain good control of Uke's head, making sure Uke is off balance and driving forward. As the sweeping action occurs with the leg, rotation of the sleeve grip turns Uke to the ground.

Opportunity for attack: This technique works better if Uke is in an upright posture about to move to his right. Harai goshi tends to be favored by taller judokas, whose height gives them effective control of their opponent's head without having to overreach.

2. Demonstrates the leg placement and upper body control.

Related techniques:

Harai makikomi (see page 44);
hane goshi (see page 38).

3. Demonstrates the sweeping
action of Tori's throwing leg.

Possible combinations and counter-techniques:

Harai goshi into osoto gake (see
page 176); harai goshi into soto
makikomi (see page 152); harai
goshi countered by ura nage (see
page 197); harai goshi countered
by ushiro goshi (see page 198).

4. Shows the continuation of the sweeping
action to complete the technique.

Harai makikomi (winding hip sweep)

Grip: Initially a high lapel and low sleeve grip is established. However, to complete this technique, the lapel grip is removed and wound round in a circular motion above Uke's right arm.

Entry and execution: As with harai goshi, the right foot initiates the entry and the left foot swings behind to become the support leg. The right leg is then brought back onto the front of Uke's thigh in a sweeping action. The lapel grip is then removed. It is the change of grip that

1. Shows the sleeve and first attack position of the winding arm.

2. Demonstrates the leg and body position for the start of the rotation.

transforms what would be harai goshi into harai makikomi. As a result of this change of grip, greater body contact is achieved and a winding action is adopted to complete the move. The technique is completed with a sweeping action with the right leg and a winding action of the body to the ground.

Opportunity for attack: This technique works well when Uke is preventing Tori from gaining a right-handed lapel grip and/or is controlling the left sleeve. It can be used as a follow-on from a blocked harai goshi.

Related techniques: Hane makikomi (see page 40); osoto makikomi (see page 84); soto makikomi (see page 98); uchimata makikomi (see page 124); harai goshi (see page 42).

3. Shows the sweeping motion of the throwing leg and rotation of the arm and body to complete the technique.

1. Shows the high lapel and low sleeve grip.

2. Shows the step sequence required. Uke is stepping back, so there is weight transference onto the back leg.

Harai tsurikomi ashi (lift-pull foot sweep)

Grip: The most effective grip for this technique is a middle lapel and low sleeve grip.

Entry and execution: This throw often takes considerable practice and perseverance to perfect, and accurate timing is imperative. Tori steps forward with the right foot. His body does not turn but remains facing Uke. As Uke starts to step backward with his right foot, Tori brings his front foot in contact

3. begin the sweep.

with the front of Uke's ankle. The lifting action of the arms and sweeping action of the leg are simultaneous. Tori pulls around firmly with the right sleeve grip, turns his head to his left shoulder and rotates Uke's body.

Opportunity for attack: This technique works best if Uke has an upright posture. Harai tsurikomi ashi can be used as a counter when Uke has attempted a forward technique, but failed and is turning back out of the technique.

Related techniques: Okuriashi barai (see page 76); sasae tsurikomi ashi (see page 92); deashi barai (see page 36).

4. Demonstrates the sweeping action required.

5. Shows Tori's maintenance of the grip to ensure that Uke lands on his back to complete the technique.

Hiza guruma (knee wheel)

Grip: A high lapel and low sleeve, or a middle lapel and low sleeve grip can be used for this move. This throw is effective when done either left- or right-footed without any change to the grip.

Entry and execution: Using a standard right-handed lapel and sleeve grip, Tori steps to the side with her right leg and props Uke's knee, just below the kneecap, with her left foot. Tori pulls Uke's right sleeve around in a large

1. Shows the high lapel and low sleeve grip and Uke's upright stance.

transverse circular motion, pulling Uke over Tori's propping leg to Uke's front right corner. Executing a left throw from a right-handed grip requires a high lapel and low sleeve grip. The objective is for Tori to step to her left with her left foot and place her right foot on the front or side of Uke's knee area, just below the kneecap. Tori then pushes Uke's arm and rotates the lapel grip to rotate Uke to the ground.

If timed correctly, Uke is unable to bend his knees in a defensive posture because Tori's foot pushes against the knee area. It is important that Tori does not lean backward when performing this technique, as she will be vulnerable to being countered.

2. Shows the foot placement on the side of Uke's knee.

3. Shows the hand control and rotation required to complete the technique.

Opportunity for attack:

This technique is most effective
when Uke moves in a semicircle to the
left or right, but can also be used when Uke is still.

Related technique: Sasae tsurikomi ashi (see page 92).

Possible combinations and counter-techniques: Hiza guruma into harai goshi (see page 154);
Hiza guruma into osoto gari (see page 177); Hiza guruma countered by ouchi gari (see page 199).

Ippon seoi nage
(one-arm shoulder throw)

Grip: There are several ways of gripping for ippon seoi nage. Tori can start with a double middle lapel grip or a middle lapel, low sleeve grip, but ultimately Tori's right arm is placed under Uke's right armpit. Tori's other hand can be attached to Uke's sleeve or lapel.

1. Shows the low sleeve grip on the arm to be attacked.

2. Demonstrates the arm placement and body position required.

Entry and execution: Ippon seoi nage is a very versatile throw, combining well with many other techniques. Tori takes a two-step entry, stepping forward with his right foot and swinging the left foot behind. His feet are approximately shoulder-width apart. Tori's back remains straight as his knees are bent, bringing his waist below Uke's. Uke's belt level is a good guideline, the aim is for Tori's belt level to be lower than Uke's. Tori places his right arm under Uke's right armpit, with the inner elbow joint in Uke's armpit region; this arm is used as a prop. Tori pulls Uke onto his back, using either a sleeve or lapel grip, then straightens his legs and rotates his upper body, pulling in a big circular movement to offload Uke.

3. Shows the rotation of Tori's shoulders to complete the technique.

Opportunity for attack:

This technique works better on a Uke with a slightly bent posture. Ippon seoi nage can be adapted to work off both knees (drop-knee ippon seoi nage, see page 52).

Related technique:

Morote seoi nage (see page 68).

Possible combination techniques: Ippon seoi nage into kata guruma (see page 156); ippon seoi nage into kouchi gake (see page 178); ippon seoi nage into seoi otoshi (see page 169); ippon seoi nage into uchi makikomi (see page 158).

Drop-knee ippon seoi nage

1. Shows the low sleeve grip on the arm to be attacked.

2. Demonstrates the arm placement and body position required. Note the knee position.

When executing drop-knee ippon seoi nage, the arm positioning is the same as with ippon seoi nage, with the inner elbow joint making contact with Uke's armpit. However, the leg movement is slightly different. As Tori turns in, he drops onto his knees, pushing the feet between Uke's legs and pulling strongly on Uke's sleeve. If Uke is not taken over immediately, Tori can push off from the mat, lifting up his backside and continuing to pull hard with the sleeve to rotate Uke over. Tori also has the option of going down into a deep squat, rather than dropping to the knees. From this position, Tori can almost stand up between Uke's legs, again rotating with the arms to rotate Uke over his back to the mat.

3. Shows the drive off the knees and the rotation of the shoulders to complete the technique.

Kata guruma (shoulder wheel)

Grip: Initially a standard middle lapel and low sleeve grip is adopted, which is later transferred to grip Uke's leg.

Entry and execution: From the standard right-handed grip, Tori lets go of the middle lapel grip and grabs the inside of Uke's leg, simultaneously stepping forward with his right foot and bending his knees as he does so. Tori positions the back of his neck and shoulders

1. Shows the initial high lapel and low sleeve grip.

2. Demonstrates the hand grip requirement and the positioning of Tori's shoulders.

under Uke's arm, pulling the sleeve and positioning his body sideways. This can be done in one of two ways: either Tori steps backward, pulling Uke forward onto his shoulders, or Tori moves in toward Uke, getting underneath him. Uke's balance is broken by Tori pulling on the sleeve once underneath. Tori straightens his legs (Uke is lifted in a type of fireman's lift movement) and uses his left and right arm simultaneously to complete the technique.

Kata guruma can also be executed by letting go of the sleeve grip and using it to grip Uke's leg. In this instance, the lapel grip is essential in order to pull Uke off balance. The rest of the technique is completed as described above,

3. Demonstrates the lifting action and the direction of the throw.

using the sleeve grip. Also, in recent years, a drop-knee version of kata guruma has developed and is used effectively in competition.

Opportunity for attack: This technique works well against a Uke with an upright posture, or as Uke is stepping forward with his right leg, using Uke's momentum.

4. Shows the rotation of the shoulders and the lifting and pulling action of the hands to complete this technique.

Kibishu gaeshi (heel trip)

Grip: Initially a middle lapel and low sleeve grip are used. Tori then drops her hand to obtain a grip of Uke's heel.

1. Shows the one-handed middle lapel grip.

Entry and execution: Tori lets go of Uke's sleeve and drops down, grabbing the inside of Uke's left heel, pulling forward with the heel grip. Tori endeavors to get Uke's sleeve as low as possible before attempting this throw. Uke is driven backward.

2. Demonstrates the hand placement on Uke's heel while maintaining the lapel grip.

Opportunity for attack:

This technique works more effectively against an opponent with a bent posture. For this technique to be most effective, it is important to catch Uke off guard with a sudden dropping action.

3. Shows the scooping action on Uke's ankle or heel and the driving motion to Uke's rear to complete this technique.

Koshi guruma (hip wheel)

Grip: Initially a low sleeve and middle lapel grip are adopted, then the lapel grip is released and the right arm is wrapped around Uke's neck.

Entry and execution: Tori steps first the right then the left foot in, using a two-step entry. Keeping hold of the lapel, Tori uses a sliding action to place her right hand behind Uke's neck. The crook of Tori's arm eventually applies pressure to the back of Uke's neck, pulling down for chest contact. The hips are in such a position that Uke's body is wheeled over Tori's hips. Very little knee bending occurs: quite often, Tori's hips will be way above Uke's.

Opportunity for attack: This technique works more effectively against an opponent with a bent posture. For this technique to most effective it is important to catch Uke off guard with a sudden dropping action.

Related technique: Ogoshi (see page 72).

1. Shows the single-hand sleeve grip with Tori's other hand not holding.

2. Demonstrates the arm placement around Uke's head and the hip and body positioning.

3. Shows the rotation required to complete the technique.

Kosoto gake
(minor outer hook)

1. Shows the high lapel and low sleeve grip and Uke's forward foot placement.

2. Shows the leg position and the breaking of Uke's balance.

Grip: The most effective grip for this technique is a middle to high lapel and low sleeve grip. Sometimes a bear-hug type grip is used to control Uke's upper body.

Entry and execution: Tori hooks his right leg around the back of Uke's left leg. The control of the sleeve prevents Uke from turning out. The power and drive of this throw comes predominantly from Tori's back (left) leg. Tori's front leg just maintains the control of Uke. It is important that Tori's hips are not too high: he should try to drop his weight as he drives Uke backward, otherwise Tori runs the risk of being countered. In order to maintain control of Uke, Tori falls forward and usually lands on top of Uke. This technique is particularly susceptible to an uchimata counter (see page 122). Therefore, it is unadvisable to attempt this technique on a known uchimata specialist.

Opportunity for attack: As Uke steps forward with the left leg, Tori should seize the opportunity to attack.

Related technique: Kosoto gari (see page 60).

3. Demonstrates the importance of the hand control and driving action required to complete this technique.

Kosoto gari (minor outer reap)

Grip: The most effective grip for this technique is a middle to high lapel and low sleeve grip.

Entry and execution: Usually a one-step entry is used. The sole of Tori's right foot connects on Uke's heel, to the outside of Uke's left leg, and sweeps in the direction of Uke's toes. The hands

1. Shows the grip and Uke's forward foot placement.

2. Demonstrates the foot placement and hand control.

control Uke and prevent her from trying to turn out, ensuring that Uke's body weight is pulled over the removed leg, causing her to lose balance and fall backward onto the mat.

Opportunity for attack:

Opportunity for this technique arises if Uke is slightly sideways on and steps forward with her left foot. Tori can also create his own opportunity by adjusting himself accordingly to carry out the technique.

3. Shows the sweeping action and hand control required to complete this technique.

Related technique: Kosoto gake (see page 58).

Possible combinations and counter-techniques: Kosoto gari into tani otoshi (see page 159); kosoto gari countered by uchimata (page 200).

Kouchi gake (minor inner hook)

Grip: The most effective grip for this technique is a middle lapel and low sleeve grip. The lapel grip is later transferred to clasp around Uke's thigh.

1. Shows Tori's initial grip.

2. Demonstrates the leg position with Tori clamping Uke's leg with his arm, which can resist the throw.

Entry and execution: Usually a one-step entry is used. Tori makes a lunging action, stepping through Uke's legs with his right leg proceeding directly to the hook, making contact with the back of Uke's right knee or calf muscle. Tori lets go with his right hand and drops his arm under Uke's right arm and holds Uke's thigh, preventing Uke from stepping off the technique. Tori drives off the back leg, maintaining his grip, and pushes his hips to the ground. Such is the technique that, to complete the throw, both Uke and Tori fall to the mat.

Opportunity for attack: Kouchi gake can be utilized when Uke is standing still with her feet apart, and can be performed either when Uke is upright or bent over. It works well if Tori pulls Uke forward with the sleeve grip and then attacks the advanced leg.

Related technique: Kouchi gari (see page 64).

3. Shows the drive off the back leg required to complete this technique.

Kouchi gari (minor inner reap)

Grip: The most effective grip for this technique is a middle lapel and low sleeve grip.

Entry and execution: Normally a one-step entry is used. Tori pushes down and backward, simultaneously sweeping Uke's right leg. The sole of Tori's right foot connects with Uke's heel. Tori sweeps in the direction Uke's toes are

1. Shows the middle lapel and low sleeve grip.

2. Demonstrates the foot placement and pulling action of the hands. Note the sole of Tori's foot in contact with Uke's heel.

facing, maintaining control with the grip and pulling down and around on Uke's sleeve.

Kouchi gari is often used to readjust the stance of one's opponent to set him or her up for various other techniques such as ippon seoi nage and tai otoshi. The "minor" in its name does not suggest that this is an inferior technique. In fact, many contests are won by an ippon-scoring kouchi gari: the "minor" simply refers to the size of the reaping movement.

3. Shows the sweeping action of Tori's foot or leg required to complete this technique.

Opportunity for attack: This technique is usually used when Uke has her weight on the back leg.

Related techniques: Morote gari (see page 66) or te otoshi (see page 112).

Possible combinations and counter-techniques: Kouchi gari into ippon seoi nage (see page 180); kouchi gari into tai otoshi (see page 182); kouchi gari countered by harai tsurikomi ashi (see page 201).

1. Shows the non-gripping stance required.

Morote gari (double leg grab)

Grip: For this move, Tori's hands go behind both of Uke's knees, usually in a cupping action rather than an actual grip.

Entry and execution: Morote gari is often referred to as the "rugby tackle" technique, as it is very similar in principle. Although simple in execution, this technique can be very effective at high-standard competitions. It is most successful when Uke is caught off guard. Before grips are established, Tori feints his hand movement toward Uke's head; this distracts Uke, making her expect a high lapel grip. Tori immediately drops his hands and bends low, by-passing Uke's hands and cupping his hands behind Uke's knees. Tori puts his head to one side of Uke's body. Then, with a straight back and bent knees, Tori lifts Uke from the mat and drives her backward. However, if Uke is particularly heavy or strongly resists, Tori simply pulls his legs

2. Shows the hand placement and lifting action.

toward himself and drives forward with his shoulder, thereby pushing Uke backward over her own legs. Some of the more spectacular morote gari throws use a lifting and turning action. Tori controls Uke's struggle to turn out in mid-air, steering Uke's hips and ensuring Uke's back hits the ground, maximizing scoring potential, ultimately for ippon.

Opportunity for attack: This technique is particularly effective against taller and/or more upright opponents. It is often used at the beginning of a contest or after a matte situation when the contest has recommenced, but before grips have been established.

Related technique: sukui nage (see page 100).

3. Tori drives Uke to the rear to complete this technique.

Morote seoi nage (two-handed shoulder throw)

Grip: The most effective grip for this technique is a middle lapel and low sleeve grip. Some judokas find it easier to grip slightly lower on the lapel, allowing enough slack in the jacket to push an elbow through.

1. Shows the middle lapel and low sleeve grip. Note Tori's lapel arm inside.

2. Shows the body placement required and the start of the lifting action. Note the elbow placement.

Entry and execution: Using a two-step entry, Tori steps his right foot forward, swinging the left foot behind so that his feet are approximately shoulder-width apart and knees are bent. Simultaneously Tori lifts Uke's right sleeve and, maintaining the middle lapel grip, pushes his elbow across and under Uke's armpit. Tori bends slightly forward as he does so, which brings Uke up onto her toes and off balance. Completion of the throw is achieved by Tori straightening his knees and rotating his upper body and head to off-load Uke.

3. Shows the rotation of Tori's shoulders required to complete this technique.

Opportunity for attack: This is most effective when Uke is in an upright posture.

Related technique: Ippon seoi nage (see page 50).

Possible combination techniques: Morote seoi nage into seoi otoshi.

Nidan kosoto gake (two-step minor outer hook)

Grip: The most effective grip for this technique is a middle lapel and low sleeve grip.

Entry and execution: Tori stands to Uke's left side. Instead of attacking Uke's left heel as with kosoto gari, Tori immediately reaches her leg across attacking the right heel. Tori uses her right leg in a scooping action, pushing down with her right arm and up with her left arm and driving Uke backward.

1. Shows the grip.

2. Shows the placement of the hooking leg.

3. Shows the driving action of Tori's back leg to complete this throw.

Opportunity for attack: This is most effective when Uke is in an upright posture and standing slightly sideways on to Tori.

Related techniques: Kosoto gake (see page 58); kosoto gari (see page 60); nidan kosoto gari (see page 71).

Nidan kosoto gari (two-step minor outer reap)

Grip: The most effective grip for this technique is a mid-lapel and low sleeve grip.

Entry and execution: Nidan kosoto gari is very similar to nidan kosoto gake. Tori stands to Uke's left side and reaches his leg across attacking Uke's right heel in a similar action to kosoto gari. The sweeping action takes both feet forward. This technique can also be used as a follow-on from a failed osoto gari (see page 80). The osoto gari attack is nullified, so the sweeping leg for the osoto gari is placed on the mat and becomes the supporting leg. Tori then uses his other leg to sweep Uke's supporting leg away.

1. Shows the mid-lapel and low sleeve grip.

Opportunity for attack: This is most effective when Uke is in an upright posture and standing slightly sideways to Tori.

Related techniques: Kosoto gari (see page 60) kosoto gake (see page 58); nidan kosoto gake (see page 70).

3. Shows the sweeping action of Tori's foot and leg to complete this throw.

2. Shows the foot placement. Note the sole of Tori's foot on Uke's heel.

Ogoshi (major hip throw)

Grip: Tori has the option of taking a standard sleeve and lapel grip and later releasing the lapel grip to hold Uke's waist. Alternatively Tori can take a low sleeve and waist grip directly.

Entry and execution: Tori takes a two-step entry, placing his backside in front of Uke's hips and sliding his arm under Uke's left arm. Tori can grip the belt, but the technique is just as effective if Tori places the palm of his hand on Uke's back.

This also ensures that Tori does not receive a penalty for holding onto the belt for too long.

1. Shows the direct grip to the waist with a low sleeve grip.

2. Shows the hip placement and the start of the lifting action.

Tori bends his knees to lower his waist below Uke's, pulling Uke onto his hip. Tori then straightens his legs and as Uke's feet leave the ground Tori rotates his upper body and head, and pulls Uke's sleeve in a transverse circular motion.

Ogoshi is very similar to uki goshi. The difference between the two techniques has to do with the amount of hip contact. Ogoshi requires a greater turn of the hips, a deeper knee bend and maximum hip contact, whereas uki goshi requires very little knee bend or hip contact and Tori is in more of a side-on position.

Opportunity for attack: This is most effective when Uke takes a high lapel grip and is upright in stance

Related techniques: Uki goshi (see page 128) and koshi guruma (see page 57).

Possible combination techniques: Ogoshi into uki goshi (see page 160).

3. Shows the rotation of and direction of the throw as it is completed.

Oguruma (major wheel)

Grip: The most effective grip for this technique is a high lapel or over-the-shoulder grip and low sleeve grip. The technique can also be applied using a double lapel grip. However, there is slightly less control, and this gives Uke more opportunity to block the technique or avoid the ippon score, as the arms are not being controlled.

Entry and execution: Using a one-step action, and standing slightly off center, Tori spins, pivoting on the left leg and placing the right leg across in front of Uke. Alternatively, Tori can adopt a two-step action by stepping the left leg forward and across in front of Uke.

1. Shows the grip with Tori extending Uke's sleeve.

(Uke is likely to be braced against the perceived attack, but this only adds to the success of this technique.) Tori spins and blocks Uke's body with a straight leg to the front of Uke's thighs, making contact with Uke just above the knee. Tori's toes should be pointed and Tori's head and leg should be parallel. Rotation of the body and head completes the technique. There is very little sweeping action from the leg.

2. Shows Tori's step pattern across his own body.

3. Demonstrates the position of the blocking leg.

Opportunity for attack: This is most effective when Uke is upright and has a slightly sideways-on stance. It works well when on the move, but can also be applied when Uke is still. It can be used against an opponent who has straight arms.

Related techniques: Ashi guruma (see page 34); harai makikomi (see page 44); osoto makikomi (see page 84); soto makikomi (see page 98); uchimata makikomi (see page 124); hane goshi (see page 38).

4. Shows how Tori rotates his shoulders to complete this technique and rotates Uke over his blocking leg.

Okuriashi barai/harai (double foot sweep)

1. Shows the middle
lapel and low sleeve grip.

Grip: The most effective grip for this technique is a high lapel and low sleeve grip.

Entry and execution: As with all foot sweeps, okuriashi barai/harai works best if Uke is in motion. Using a one-step action, Tori places the sole of the foot to the side of Uke's foot. The sweeping action pushes one of Uke's feet into the other. Tori's hands direct Uke down to the mat.

2. Shows how Tori sweeps one of Uke's legs into the other while taking Uke's upper body off balance.

Opportunity for attack:

Okuriashi barai/harai is most successful when Uke is skipping sideways or moving in a semicircle.

Related technique: Deashi barai/harai (see page 36).

3. Shows the sweeping action of the foot and leg, which completes the throw.

Possible combinations and counter-techniques: Okuriashi barai/harai countered by tsubame gaeshi (see page 203).

Osoto gake (major outer hook)

1. Shows the high lapel and low sleeve grip.

Grip: The most effective grip for this technique is a high lapel and low sleeve grip.

2. Demonstrates the throwing position.

Entry and execution: Usually a one-step entry is used. Tori drives with her right leg to the back of Uke's right leg, endeavoring to hook the back of Uke's knee. The power of the drive comes from the back leg. The high lapel grip controls Uke's head. A hopping action can be used, while continuing the drive, to bring Tori's supporting leg closer, if necessary.

Opportunity for attack: Osoto gake works best when Uke's right leg is still, or he is about to step forward.

Related technique: Osoto gari (page 90).

Possible combinations and counter-techniques: Osoto gake into osoto gari (see page 161); osoto gake to seoi otoshi (see page 185).

3. Shows the standing leg position.

4. Shows the throwing leg lifting Uke to complete this technique.

Osoto gari (major outer reap)

Grip: The most effective grip for this technique is a high lapel and low sleeve grip, although a mid-lapel and low sleeve grip can also be effective.

1. Shows the high lapel and low sleeve grip.

Entry and execution: Initially Tori steps forward with her left leg toward Uke's right foot, placing her left foot level or just past Uke's right foot. (Tori allows enough space for her right leg to go through between the outside of Uke's right leg and Tori's own left leg.) Tori's hips should be slightly rotated and hooking the back of Uke's thigh. The sweeping action is executed following the breaking of balance to Uke's rear right corner. Tori's head and the heel of her sweeping leg should be parallel; therefore, the lower the head, the higher the heel should go. To complete the technique, Tori's right leg connects with

2. Shows the first step and the breaking of balance to Uke's rear.

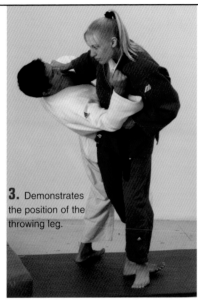

the back of Uke's right leg and Tori lowers her head and drives back and down with her hands.

Opportunity for attack: Osoto gari is most successful against an opponent with an upright posture and when Uke's feet are level or the attacked leg is slightly back.

Related technique: Osoto gake (see page 78).

3. Demonstrates the position of the throwing leg.

Possible combinations and counter-techniques:

Osoto gari to nidan kosoto gari (see page 71);
osoto gari to yoko wakare (see page 146).

4. Shows the completion of the technique by lifting the throwing leg.

Osoto guruma (major outer wheel)

Grip: The most effective grip for this technique is a high over-the-shoulder grip or high lapel grip with a low sleeve grip.

Entry and execution: The high grip gives Tori good head control. Tori steps in with his left foot, breaking Uke's balance to his rear on the step. The

1. Shows a high over-the-shoulder grip.

right leg blocks behind both of Uke's legs; Tori's toes should be pointed. A similar action is used when executing osoto gari (see page 80) except that both legs are attacked. Tori rotates to his left. The blocking leg does not sweep; Uke is wheeled over the leg.

Opportunity for attack: This technique works best as a combination with an osoto gake attack that is continued into osoto guruma. That is, Tori attacks one, then both, of Uke's legs. This throw works well if Uke's stance is predominantly sideways-on to Tori.

2. Shows the body position required for this throw.

Related techniques: Osoto gake (see page 78); osoto gari (see page 80).

3. Shows the rotation required to complete this technique.

1. Shows the sleeve grip, with the rotational arm about to make contact.

Osoto makikomi (major outer winding)

Grip: The most effective grip for this technique is a middle lapel and low sleeve grip.

2. Demonstrates the body contact required.

Entry and execution: As a result of the similarity in name, osoto makikomi is sometimes confused with soto makikomi. However, with soto makikomi, Uke is thrown forward, whereas with osoto makikomi, Uke is thrown to the rear. Tori steps forward with her left foot and, letting go of the lapel grip, wraps her arm around Uke's lapel-grip arm and simultaneously steps behind Uke's right leg. Placing her leg on the floor, Tori rotates her body into the ground. Osoto makikomi can be made as a direct attack or as a continuation of a failed osoto gari (see page 80).

Opportunity for attack: Entry is facilitated if Uke is standing slightly sideways-on to Tori and has an upright posture.

Related techniques: Hane makikomi (see page 40); soto makikomi (see page 98); uchimata makikomi (page 124).

3. Completion of the throw is achieved by the rotation of Tori's arm and body.

Osoto otoshi (major outer drop)

Grip: The most effective grip for this technique is a high lapel and low sleeve grip.

Entry and execution: Tori steps forward with his left leg and hooks behind Uke's right leg, driving his leg and foot into the ground between Uke's legs. Tori's foot makes contact with the mat, with his leg causing Uke's leg to fold. Tori leans forward and drives, with the hands direct to the ground, to Uke's rear. No rotation is involved.

1. Shows the low sleeve grip.

2. Demonstrates the initial step and shows the chest control.

3. Shows the body contact and the leg block required.

Opportunity for attack: This works well if Uke is standing slightly sideways-on and has a middle lapel grip. This technique is linked with osoto gake. There are similarities in the execution of these techniques (predominantly the hook and drive back).

Related technique: Osoto gake (see page 78).

4. Shows the rotation required to complete the technique.

Ouchi gake (major inner hook)

Grip: The most effective grip for this technique is a middle lapel and low sleeve grip.

1. Shows the middle lapel and low sleeve grip.

2. Shows the body position required, the positioning of the hooking leg and the driving leg.

Entry and execution: This requires a one-step move. Tori turns to an almost side-on position and drives the right leg behind Uke's calf, or back of the knee, into a hook position. The hips are turned forward. Tori drives down and back with his arms. The right leg clamps Uke's leg and the standing leg performs a driving action, taking Uke directly to the rear.

Opportunity for attack: Ouchi gake works well against a bent, defensive posture in an Uke with a wide stance. It can work well if used with combination techniques, for example, a forward throw into a backward throw.

Related technique: Ouchi gari (see page 90).

3. Emphasizes the hand control on the lapel grip that is required to complete this throw.

Ouchi gari (major inner reap)

Grip: The most effective grip for this technique is a middle lapel and low sleeve grip.

Entry and execution: This throw works on a three-step entry, although a one-step entry is possible. With the three-step entry, Tori steps forward with his right foot, swinging his left leg behind and positioning it behind the heel of his right foot. Then Tori positions his right leg on the calf of Uke's left leg and simultaneously pushes back and down with the lapel hand, converting Uke's weight over the leg to be attacked. Tori should aim to put his head over Uke's right shoulder, that is, on the opposite side to which Tori's leg attacks. This

1. Shows the middle lapel controlling Uke's chest.

2. Shows the first step and breaking of balance.

3. Shows the second step, where Uke makes a half circle to Tori's rear.

reduces the risk of being countered. It is also important not to lean backward when attempting this throw, as Tori runs the risk of being countered by such techniques as ouchi gaeshi or kosoto gari. Tori moves his right leg in a semicircular action and drives Uke's body down to the ground with the right hand.

Sometimes Uke is able to maintain her balance. In this instance, Tori should persevere by hopping toward Uke on his supporting leg and continuing the reaping action of the right leg and the downward pull on Uke's sleeve. This can then become more of an ouchi gake.

Ouchi gari is very useful as part of a combination or when it is used as a feint to cause Uke to react and therefore change her stance, setting him up for another throw.

4. Demonstrates the reaping leg position.

5. Shows the reaping action required to complete this technique.

Opportunity for attack:

Ouchi gari works best when Uke is square-on and with a wide stance, or about to step forward with his left leg.

Related technique:

Ouchi gake (see page 88).

Possible combinations and counter-techniques: Ouchi gari into kosoto gake (see page 164); ouchi gari into kouchi gari (see page 166).

Sasae tsurikomi ashi (propping drawing ankle)

Grip: The most effective grip for this technique is a middle lapel and low sleeve grip.

1. Shows the correct grip.

2. Show's Tori's first step to his right.

Entry and execution: Tori steps forward to the outside of Uke's left leg. Tori stands on his right foot and brings his left foot to the front of Uke's left ankle. This action should make Uke step backward. Tori follows through with a sweeping action with his left leg. This action can result in thigh-to-thigh contact if it continues through. A large rotation, or circular motion, is required of Tori's hands to complete the technique.

Opportunity for attack: Uke is slightly sideways-on, the attacking foot is off center, and Uke is about to travel backward. This technique is particularly suitable for taller judokas, who are able to use their long limbs to their advantage.

Related techniques: Ouchi gari (see page 90); harai tsurikomi ashi (see page 46).

Possible combinations and counter-techniques: Sasae tsurikomi ashi to deashi barai (see page 188).

3. Shows the positioning of the blocking foot and the pulling action of the sleeve grip.

4. Shows the rotation of Tori's body that is required to complete this throw.

1. Shows the correct grip.

Seoi otoshi (shoulder drop)

Grip: The most effective grip for this technique is a middle lapel and low sleeve grip.

2. Shows the one-step entry, pivoting on the supporting leg.

Entry and execution: The most effective entry is usually a one-step. However, a three-step entry also works. With the one-step entry, Tori steps across, blocking Uke's right leg. Tori then rotates his hips through, simultaneously pushing his elbow under Uke's right armpit, while still maintaining the grip on Uke's left lapel. Tori rotates the shoulder to complete the technique. Tori can also place the knee of the blocking leg on the ground.

3. Demonstrates the position of the body and elbow.

Opportunity for attack: This throw works well against an upright posture, when Uke is standing still or coming forward, but invariably is used against a semi-bent posture.

Related technique:

Tai otoshi (see page 106).

4. Shows the rotation required to complete this technique.

Sode tsurikomi goshi (sleeve lift-pull hip throw)
1 Sleeve and lapel grip

1. Shows the single sleeve and middle lapel grip.

2. Shows Tori pushing the sleeve up and simultaneously stepping across the front of Uke.

3. Demonstrates the body positioning.

Grip: Tori can use a standard middle lapel and low sleeve grip or a double sleeve grip.

Entry and execution: The most effective entry is a one-step. Tori takes a standard sleeve and lapel grip. If he wanted to turn right, Tori would take a left-handed grip because, with this technique, he pushes the sleeve arm across Uke's body and anchors on the lapel. Uke is forced over Tori's hips.

Alternatively, Tori can work from both sleeves, pushing Uke's sleeve up above his shoulder line, breaking Uke's grip, then rotating his hips across. Tori pulls one sleeve down and the other up, and Uke is rotated over Tori's hips.

4. Shows the rotation required to complete both throws.

1. Shows the double sleeve grip.

2. Tori pushes Uke's sleeve up and simultaneously steps across.

2 Double sleeve grip

3. Demonstrates Tori's body positioning.

Opportunity for attack: This throw works well against a Uke with a high lapel and sleeve grip with an upright posture (Uke's grip is broken as the arm is pushed across the body).

Soto makikomi (outside winding) with leg block

Grip: Initially Tori takes a standard middle lapel and low sleeve grip. The lapel grip is later released and the right arm wraps around Uke's right arm.

Entry and execution: Soto makikomi is performed using a two-step entry. Tori steps forward with the right foot, swinging the left foot behind. At the same time she lets go of the lapel grip, wrapping the right arm around Uke's arm, pulling strongly on the sleeve grip and pushing the hips through. Tori's right leg can be used as a block, but it is not always necessary. Rotation of Tori's body goes directly into the ground. This is not to be mistaken for osoto makikomi, which is a rear technique.

1. Shows the sleeve grip with the first stage of the rotating arm.

2. Shows the blocking leg position and the second stage of the arm wrap.

3. Shows the rotation required to complete the technique.

without leg block

1. Shows the sleeve grip with the first stage of the rotating arm.

2. Shows the body positioning of Tori's hip.

3. Shows the rotation required to complete the throw.

Opportunity for attack: This technique is aided by a Uke with an upright posture, standing slightly sideways-on.

Related techniques:

Hane makikomi (see page 40); osoto makikomi (see page 84); uchimata makikomi (see page 124).

Sukui nage (scooping throw)

Grip: A middle lapel and low sleeve grip is rapidly changed to a double leg grip to either the back of the thighs or front of the trousers. Alternatively, Tori may choose to go straight to the leg grip.

1. Shows the middle lapel grip.

2. Shows Tori's body and hand positioning.

Entry and execution: Tori immediately steps behind Uke (Tori will then be facing the same direction as Uke), blocking both of Uke's legs. Grasping Uke's legs, behind the knee or gripping the cloth at the front of Uke's trousers, Tori lifts Uke and takes Uke directly back over Tori's blocking legs, pushing back with the shoulder.

3. Demonstrates the lifting action.

Opportunity for attack: This works well if Uke is predominantly sideways-on, with a high lapel grip.

Related techniques: Te guruma (see page 110); morote gari (see page 66).

4. Shows how Uke is driven onto his back to complete the technique.

Sumi gaeshi (corner throw)

Grip: Tori grips over Uke's shoulder. Tori can use a low sleeve and belt grip, although there may be many variations in gripping styles for this throw.

Entry and execution: Tori immediately steps forward with the right foot and places the front of the right foot on the inside of Uke's thigh. The action then consists of Tori falling onto his back and pulling strongly on the belt or

the back of Uke's jacket. The direction of the throw can be to Tori's left or right, or directly over Tori's head.

This technique is a sacrifice throw. Therefore, there is a danger that Uke may capitalize on Tori's technique. It is important to realize that, according to the rules laid down by the International Judo Federation (IJF), for Tori to score in competition from a sumi gaeshi

1. Shows the sleeve and over the back grip to control Uke.

attack, there must be clear separation between Tori and Uke. This however, reduces the amount of control that Tori can enforce.

Opportunity for attack: This technique is usually done against an opponent with a highly defensive posture, where Uke is bent over with his feet spread.

Related technique: tomoe nage (see page 114).

2. Demonstrates the positioning of Tori's leg.

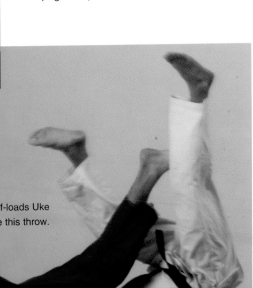

3. Tori rolls back and off-loads Uke using the leg to complete this throw.

Sumi otoshi (corner drop)

1. Shows the high lapel and low sleeve grip.

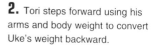

2. Tori steps forward using his arms and body weight to convert Uke's weight backward.

Grip: Tori takes a middle lapel and low sleeve grip.

Entry and execution: Using a one-step entry, Tori steps forward with his left foot, placing it to the outside of Uke, level with Uke's right foot. As he does so, Tori drives down with the sleeve grip and lifts with the lapel grip using a circling hand action. This throw is most effectively used at those times when an opponent mis-times an uchimata (see page 122)

or osoto gari (see page 80) attack, and Tori uses his momentum against them.

Opportunity for attack: This throw is used as Uke steps forward on his right foot and is a pure breaking of balance technique to Uke's right corner.

Related techniques: Kosoto gake (see page 58); kosoto gari (see page 60); nidan kosoto gari (see page 71).

3. Uke is driven onto his back by Tori's hand movement, which completes the technique.

Tai otoshi (body drop)

1. Shows the middle lapel and low sleeve grip.

2. Tori pivots on his right leg, taking his left leg back while pulling Uke off-balance with the arms.

Grip: A middle lapel and low sleeve grip are usually taken, although a variety of grips can be used.

Entry and execution: Tori can use either a three-step entry or a one-step entry for this throw. The objective is to get Tori's right leg across Uke's right leg: this leg is used as a block. When using a three-step entry, Tori steps forward with his right leg, swinging his left leg behind, and then steps across with his right leg. At the same time, Tori breaks Uke's balance to Uke's front right corner, rotating with the hands. When using the one-step entry, Tori pivots across into the same position in one rapid movement.

Opportunity for attack: This throw can be used when Uke is square-on. It works best if a middle lapel grip is on the inside, although Tori can use a variety of grips. It is a useful technique to use if Uke has a narrow stance, as Tori does not need to get in between Uke's legs to throw him.

Related technique: Seoi otoshi (see page 94).

Possible combinations: tai otoshi into uchimata (see page 170).

3. Tori steps his right leg across in front of Uke. Pushing up with his elbow and around with the sleeve.

4. Uke is driven over Tori's leg onto his back to complete this throw.

Tani otoshi (valley drop)

Grip: This throw tends to be most effective from a mid-lapel and low sleeve grip, although it can work from a variety of grips.

Entry and execution: Using a one-step entry, Tori steps behind both of Uke's legs, while throwing her body to the ground, bearing down with the lapel and sleeve grips. Tori's body weight is used to drive Uke backward and into the mat. Uke is unable to step backward and recover his balance, as Tori's leg blocks the back of both of his legs.

Opportunity for attack: This technique is usually attempted against an opponent with a defensive posture or against one standing sideways-on. However, it is very effective as a counter against an opponent who is turning in for a forward technique.

Related technique: Yoko otoshi (see page 143).

1. Shows the middle lapel and low sleeve grip.

2. Tori drops her wight, placing her leg behind Uke and maintaining the grips.

3. Uke is forced backward onto his back.

Te guruma (hand wheel)

Grip: Initially a middle to shoulder grip or middle to high lapel and low sleeve grip are used. The sleeve grip is later transferred to grip between Uke's legs.

Entry and execution: Te guruma can be used as a direct attack or as a counter. When executed as a direct attack, Tori uses a one-step entry, stepping with his left leg and simultaneously ducking his head under Uke's armpit. Tori lets go of the sleeve grip and positions his left hand on Uke's rear inside thigh, either cupping the thigh or gripping the thigh area of the trouser leg, while still maintaining the grip on Uke's lapel. Tori bends his knees, pulling Uke in close, then lifts Uke into the air and rotates him with his hands on the lapel and thigh grips.

1. Tori has a mid-shoulder and low sleeve grip.

2. Tori steps in and grasps Uke's thigh.

3. Tori uses the power of his legs to lift Uke.

4. Tori rotates Uke in the air.

5. Uke is thrown onto his back to complete the throw.

Opportunity for attack: Te guruma is usually attempted when Uke has an extreme sideways-on stance or as he turns in for an attack.

Related technique: Sukui nage (see page 100).

Te otoshi (hand drop)

Grip: Initially a traditional middle lapel and low sleeve grip are used.

Entry and execution: Tori starts with a sleeve and lapel grip. He then lets go of the sleeve grip and crosses over to Uke's sleeve, which is also Uke's lapel arm. Tori lets go of the lapel and takes his armpit over onto Uke's wrist. Bearing his weight down, he takes his hand down to the back of Uke's knee, while still maintaining the sleeve grip. He then steps as far forward as possible with the leg nearest to Uke, simultaneously throwing himself onto his own back and lifting Uke's leg, taking Uke backward onto the mat.

1. Demonstrates the cross-sleeve grip.

2. Tori takes his arm over Uke's arm and grips Uke's leg.

3. Tori leans on Uke's arm and steps through with his leg.

Opportunity for attack: Te otoshi works best when Uke's right leg is still or he is about to step forward.

Related technique: Tani otoshi (see page 108).

4. Uke is driven backward onto the mat to complete this technique.

Tomoe nage (circular throw)

1. Uke has a jigota (bent-over) posture.

Grip: Tomoe nage is executed using a mid-lapel and low sleeve grip.

Entry and execution: Tomoe nage is often referred to as the stomach throw. This technique is a rather spectacular throw when executed correctly and it is for this reason that it is often featured in fight scenes in action movies. Tomoe nage is, however, a sacrifice technique and therefore should be attempted with extreme caution: a failed tomoe nage could result in one's opponent gaining the score (usually ippon, as Tori puts herself straight onto her own back). Tori uses a one-step entry. Initially Tori places her left foot in between Uke's legs, pulling forward with the arms to break Uke's balance. Her right foot is placed on Uke's stomach at belt level and Tori drops to the mat, aiming to get her backside as close to Uke as possible. Tori pulls Uke forward onto her foot and rolls backward, taking Uke over her head.

2. Tori drops underneath Uke, pulling down on the upper body and placing her foot onto Uke's stomach.

Opportunity for attack: This

technique is ideal against a Uke with a bent posture, or if Tori's head is being pulled down.

Related technique: Sumi gaeshi
(see page 102).

3. Tori uses her hands and foot to direct Uke onto his back to complete the throw.

Tsuri goshi (fishing/lifting hip throw)

Grip: Tori takes a rear jacket or belt grip with the right hand over Uke's left or right shoulder and a low sleeve grip with the left.

Entry and execution: This technique is sometimes referred to as the "fishing hip throw." Using a two-step entry, Tori steps forward with the right leg deep between Uke's legs, swinging his left leg and placing it parallel with the right

1. Shows the belt grip.

2. Demonstrates the body position, placement of the hips and arm control.

foot. As he does so, Tori pushes his hips in front of Uke's body, normally above Uke's belt. Tori then falls forward and rotates his shoulders, wrapping the arm under.

Opportunity for attack:

This is normally attempted against an opponent with a bent, defensive posture.

3. Shows the rotation required to complete the technique.

1. Shows the grip and Uke's posture.

Tsurikomi goshi
(lift-pull hip throw)

Grip: This technique works best from a high lapel and low sleeve grip.

2. Demonstrates the body position required and the placement of the hips below Uke's waist.

Entry and execution: This technique is executed using a one-step entry involving a spring action of Tori's right leg. The leg aims for a position that is parallel to Tori's shoulders. Tori's hips are placed approximately level with Uke's hips on initial contact. Uke starts to resist by pushing the stomach forward. Tori lowers his center of gravity by bending his knees, simultaneously pulling Uke forward. Then Tori straightens his legs, driving his hips up into Uke's abdomen and pulling around strongly with the sleeve grip.

3. Shows the lifting action onto Tori's hips.

Opportunity for attack: This works against a very strong, square-on, upright Uke, with an inside lapel grip.

Possible combinations and counter-techniques:

Tsurikomi goshi countered by utsuri goshi (see page 207).

4. Shows the rotation using the hands required to complete this technique.

Uchi makikomi
(inner winding throw)

Grip: Tori has initially a low sleeve middle lapel grip, then release the lapel grip.

Entry and execution: Tori takes his arm under Uke's armpit, while swinging his non-supporting leg behind him, positioning Tori's back against Uke's chest. Both of Tori's feet are on the ground. The throw is executed by Tori stepping sideways across with his right leg. This action allows Tori to engage in a falling action, which breaks Uke's balance and

1. Shows the over-arm, middle lapel grip and the non-gripping hand start position.

2. Demonstrates the arm and body positioning.

3. Shows the foot placement of the step across action.

takes Uke toward the ground. At the same time, a winding action on Uke's held arm rotates Uke onto his back.

Opportunity for attack: Uke in an upright posture, square-on with a middle lapel and low sleeve grip on Tori

Related techniques: Ippon seoi nage (page 50); osoto-makikomi (page 84).

4. Shows the shoulder rotation required to complete the throw.

1. Shows the high collar grip and Uke's half-bent stance.

Entry and execution:

Uchimata is a very effective technique, but it takes some time to master it properly. Uchimata is frequently performed using a three-step entry, although it is possible to execute from a one-step entry. Using a three-step entry, Tori steps forward with his right foot, placing the foot well between Uke's legs. The left leg rotates behind and is placed as close as possible to Tori's right foot to become the supporting leg. Tori's right leg then lifts between Uke's legs, making contact with the inside of Uke's thigh. Tori's

Uchimata (inner thigh throw)

Grip: This throw is very effective using a high collar and low sleeve grip. However, it can also work with a middle lapel and low sleeve grip.

2. Demonstrates the first-step placement of the right foot.

3. Shows the second-step placement of the support foot.

well against a Uke with a high lapel and sleeve grip with an upright posture.

Related technique:
Hane goshi (see page 38).

Possible combinations:
Tai otoshi into uchimata (see page 170).

head remains parallel with his own leg. Tori pulls in with the arms to maintain chest contact, and rotates his body. There are numerous variations to uchimata: it can be performed as a hip technique (as described above) or as more of a leg technique involving a hopping action, and it is often successfully paired with ouchi gari (see page 90). It is a very useful technique, as it works well against an opponent with a bent posture. As with all techniques, one should be aware of the risk of a counter.

Opportunity for attack: This throw works

4. Shows the third position of the lifting leg and Tori's rotation to complete the technique.

Uchimata makikomi (winding inner-thigh throw)

Grip: Initially a high lapel and low sleeve grip are taken. The lapel grip is then removed and the arm is taken over Uke's right arm in a winding action.

Entry and execution: Uchimata makikomi is most successful using a three-step entry. For her first step, Tori puts her right foot between Uke's legs. The second step brings the left leg behind and rotates Tori's body, and for the third step, Tori lifts her leg between Uke's. As Tori lifts her leg, she lets go of the lapel and wraps the loose arm around Uke's right arm,

1. Shows the single sleeve grip with the first stage of the winding arm.

2. Demonstrates the position of the throwing leg and the winding action against the sleeve.

maintaining the low sleeve grip. The lift takes place and Tori lowers her head toward the ground, at the same time rotating her head and body and wrapping her arm around.

Opportunity for attack: This throw works best against an opponent with a bent posture. It can also be done as a combination with uchimata: as Uke blocks an uchimata attempt, Tori carries on into uchimata makikomi. Or it can be used as a direct attack with Uke standing still and square-on.

Related techniques: Uchimata (see page 122); other makikomi techniques (see pages 44, 84, 98).

3. Shows the level of rotation required to complete the technique.

Ude gaeshi (arm roll)

Grip: Tori grips as Uke is about to take a lapel grip. Tori grips Uke's wrist with his right hand and the left hand takes a grip under Uke's left armpit.

Entry and execution: As Uke steps forward, Tori grips as described above. This technique uses a one-step entry. Tori steps

1. Shows the grip on the wrist and under Uke's armpit.

2. Demonstrates the sidestep foot placement.

across with his right leg to the side of Uke, throwing his body to the ground (and sacrificing his upright stance). Tori then continues rotation, pushing the wrist grip up into Uke's abdomen.

Opportunity for attack: This technique works when Uke is attempting to grip the lapel, with a sideways stance.

Related technique:

Sumi gaeshi (see page 102).

3. Shows the fall and rotation required to complete the throw.

Uki goshi (floating hip throw)

Grip: Tori initially grips the middle lapel and low on the sleeve. Tori then lets go and takes his arm around Uke's waist.

Entry and execution: The step pattern for this throw is normally one-step. Tori's right leg steps across the front of Uke and is placed in

1. Shows Tori's sleeve and waist grip.

2. Demonstrates the hip placement and arm grip.

the middle of Uke's feet. Meanwhile, Tori's hip is positioned in the middle of Uke's abdomen and the right arm slides around Uke's waist. The throwing action, rather than a lifting action, which occurs with techniques such as ogoshi, is more of a pulling action around the hip placement.

Opportunity for attack: A good time to use this throw is when Uke is upright and standing predominantly sideways onto Tori.

Related technique: Ogoshi (see page 72).

3. Shows the hip rotation required to complete the technique.

Uki otoshi (floating drop)

Grip: Tori uses a middle lapel and low sleeve grip.

Entry and execution: Using a one-step action, Tori steps back with her left leg, going down onto her knee. As she does so, she pulls Uke to her front right corner, driving up with the right lapel hand and then rotating the hands in order to break Uke's balance.

Opportunity for attack: This is used when Uke is stepping forward, normally from a square-on position and an upright posture.

1. Shows the grip.

2. Shows the hand action breaking Uke's balance. Tori begins to step back.

3. Tori completes the throw by going down onto one knee and rotating her hands.

Uki waza (floating throw)

Grip: Tori takes a middle lapel and low sleeve grip.

Entry and execution: This technique consists of a one-step entry, where Tori steps across in front of Uke with her left leg, placing the whole leg in front of Uke, and throws herself into a sitting position. Tori pulls the sleeve down and drives up with the right arm. There is no contact between Uke and Tori except the hands and possibly Uke's ankle briefly touching Tori's thigh. This technique uses one's opponent's forward motion against him.

1. Shows the grip.

2. Shows the leg and body placement required.

Opportunity for attack: This technique should be attempted as Uke is stepping forward with his right leg and just as his weight shifts onto the front stepping leg.

3. Shows the direction in which Uke is thrown with the hands to complete the technique.

Ura nage (rear throw)

Grip: Initially Tori grips the middle of the lapel and low on the sleeve. Tori later transfers the lapel grip to a grip around Uke's waist.

1. Shows the low sleeve grip and the release of the lapel grip.

Entry and execution: This throw is normally executed as a counter throw. Tori initially grips mid-lapel and low sleeve as Uke attempts a forward throw. Tori releases his grip on the sleeve placing his arm around to the front of Uke's waist. Tori then bends his knees to lower his hips and pulls Uke back to make body contact. With a lifting action he falls back, simultaneously throwing Uke over his right shoulder (to his back right corner).

2. Demonstrates the arm and hip placement.

Opportunity for attack: This technique is used as Uke attacks, usually with a hip throw.

Related technique: Ushiro goshi (see page 134).

3. Demonstrates the lifting action.

4. Shows the direction in which Uke is thrown with the rotation required to complete the throw.

Ushiro goshi (rear hip throw)

Grip: Tori initially grips the middle lapel and low on the sleeve. Tori then lets go and takes his arm around Uke's hips/waist.

Entry and execution: This throw is generally used as a counter. As Uke attacks, Tori lets go of the lapel. The lapel grip is converted into a hip grip, to the front of Uke's hips, with Tori pulling Uke toward himself to make body contact. Tori bends his knees, dropping his hips below Uke's. Then, with a thrusting action of his hips, Tori pushes Uke's body away and Uke drops on his back to the front of Tori. There is no twisting action involved.

1. Shows the first grip.

2. Demonstrates the arm and hip placement.

3. Shows the lifting action.

Opportunity for attack: This throw is used as Uke attacks with a forward throw. It can also be used as a counter to a semi-executed osoto gake, harai goshi, or other hip technique.

Related technique: Ura nage (see page 132).

4. Shows the direction of the throw that completes this technique.

1. Shows the arm around the waist grip and hip placement.

Utsuri goshi (hip transfer throw)

Grip: Tori initially grips the middle lapel and low on the lapel. Tori then lets go and takes his arm around Uke's waist.

Entry and execution: This is a counter throw. As Uke turns in for a hip throw, Tori lets go of the lapel grip and places his arm around Uke's waist. He blocks Uke's initial entry, bends his knees, drops his hips below Uke's, and pulls Uke's body on, lifting Uke by straightening the legs. Tori initiates a thrusting action, which pushes Uke away. Tori then steps forward with his right leg, placing his hips in front of Uke's. Uke falls onto Tori's hips.

2. Demonstrates the lifting action.

Uke is then rotated as in the execution of ogoshi.

Opportunity for attack: A good time to use this throw is when Uke is attacking with a hip technique that is only partially executed.

Related techniques: Ogoshi (see page 72); ushiro goshi (see page 134).

3. Shows the second hip and arm placement.

4. Shows the rotation of Uke to the mat, which completes the technique.

Yama arashi (mountain storm)

Grip: Initially a standard sleeve and lapel grip are used. The lapel hand is then moved to hold the same side lapel as the sleeve grip.

1. Shows the initial sleeve and lapel grip.

2. Demonstrates the body and hand position.

3. Shows the lifting action of the sweeping leg.

Entry and execution: This technique was specifically devised to allow a smaller person to beat larger opponents. The entry is a one-step entry. Tori swings across, simultaneously pulling Uke into body contact. The blocking leg is placed across the front of Uke's thighs. Using a lifting action of the arms and leg at the same time, Tori rotates his body.

Opportunity for attack: This technique is normally executed against an opponent with an upright, square-on posture.

Related techniques: Ashi guruma (see page 34); harai goshi (see page 42); oguruma (see page 74).

4. Shows the rotation required with the hands and the fully extended leg, which completes this throw.

Yoko gake (side hook)

1. Shows the grip. Uke's foot is slightly forward.

Grip: Tori establishes a mid-lapel and low sleeve grip.

Entry and execution: The entry is a two-step entry. Tori swings his left leg behind his own body, bringing himself parallel with Uke. Tori then places his right foot on his heel and lifts his leg, at the same time falling backward (sacrifice).

Opportunity for attack: This technique works best if Uke has an upright posture and is standing sideways-on.

Related techniques: Kosoto gaki (see page 58); kosoto gari (see page 60).

2. Demonstrates the placement of Tori's foot.

3. Shows the lifting action of the throwing leg, which completes this throw.

Yoko guruma
(side wheel)

Grip: Tori takes a mid-lapel and low sleeve grip.

Entry and execution: The step pattern for entry is one-step. Tori swings his leg through Uke's legs and throws his body to the ground in front of Uke, pulling Uke's body over the swinging leg.

Opportunity for attack: This throw works best against an opponent who is predominantly sideways-on. It can be used as a counter to a hip technique.

1. Shows the mid-lapel and low sleeve grip.

2. Shows the first foot placement.

3. Demonstrates the body position.

4. Shows the direction of the throw and the pull of the hands to complete this technique.

Yoko otoshi (side drop)

Grip: Tori takes a middle lapel and low sleeve grip.

Entry and execution: The entry is a one-step. Tori steps forward with his left leg and throws himself to the ground while pulling down on the sleeve. To be effective, the drop to the ground needs to be a sudden movement. Normally body contact is only between the hands and legs.

Opportunity for attack: This is used when Uke has a sideways-on stance and his front leg is weight-bearing.

1. Shows the mid-lapel and low sleeve grip.

2. Tori steps forward with his left leg.

3. Demonstrates the body position.

4. This shows the direction of the throw. Tori uses his hands to complete the technique.

Yoko sutemi waza (side sacrifice technique)

Grip: Tori takes a traditional mid-lapel and low sleeve grip, changing the sleeve grip and placing it on the sleeve of the lapel-grip arm.

2. Tori places his leg on Uke's far leg.

1. Tori grips Uke's sleeve and over Uke's back.

Entry and execution:

Uke takes a traditional right-handed grip, then reaches across and takes Uke's sleeve on the lapel-grip arm. He pushes his arm around Uke's upper back, pulling Uke into him and stepping forward with his left leg. Tori leaves his right leg blocking Uke's right leg, and makes a circular action with his upper back grip. Instead of placing his leg as a block to Uke's outer leg, Tori could put the leg inside in an uchimata action (see page 122) and switch into a sumi gaeshi action (see page 102).

3. Demonstrates Tori's falling action.

Opportunity for attack: This works well when Uke is standing sideways-on with a single lapel grip pushing Tori away.

Related techniques: Sumi gaeshi (see page 102); other sacrifice techniques (see pages 98, 131, 143).

4. Shows the direction of the throw.

1. Shows the lapel grip and the release of the sleeve grip.

Yoko wakari (side separation)

Grip: Tori takes a middle lapel and low sleeve grip and later the release of the sleeve grip.

Entry and execution: The entry is a one-step entry. Stepping deep across Uke's posture, Tori simultaneously lets go of the lapel grip and wraps his

arm under Uke's armpit. Tori initially throws herself toward the ground as if going to land on her back. However, before contact is made between Tori's body and the ground, Tori spins to face down, ideally pulling Uke over onto his back.

Opportunity for attack: This throw works best against an opponent with a high lapel grip, pulling Tori's head down and standing square on.

Related techniques: Ude gaeshit and luki waza; other sacrifice techniques (see pages 44, 102, 132).

2. Shows the placement of Tori's arm and leg, and the falling action of Tori's body.

3. Shows the rotation required to complete the technique.

chapter 3

Tachi waza (combination and counter-techniques)

If a judoka were to use the same technique all the time, he or she would become predictable and easy to defeat through a counter-maneuver. There is a need, therefore, for a judoka constantly to add to his or her repertoire by combining one technique with another or more.

All the techniques shown in this book can be used in combination and are referred to by the group names, renzoku waza (see pages 151–171) and renraku waza (see pages 172–191). The objective is to employ the principle that any action creates a reaction. Therefore, if Tori attacks Uke, Uke will either defend or block against it, will move away from it, or will have to change his stance in expectation of an attack. Different techniques are then combined to capitalize on the way Uke moves.

The combinations demonstrated here are generally one technique into another. However, a judoka may link two, three, or four techniques together in an attempt to out-wit an opponent. Equally, combinations do not necessarily follow-on from each other, but become a successive run of one judoka countering the action of the other, and so on. A good judoka will be able to accomplish instantaneous explosive techniques, but will also use combination and counter-techniques to add an element of successful unpredictability.

There are three tactics involved in using combination techniques:

Body contact waza

Tori attacks to achieve body contact, and maintains contact as Uke resists and reacts. Tori moves to the second waza, as Uke's resistance has placed his body in a more unstable position.

A feint

This combination requires Tori to make an action that sets his opponent up for a certain throw, while actually moving into another. The feint must be convincing, otherwise the essential

element of surprise will be lost. Another way a feint can be used to provoke a reaction is for Tori just to pull or push forward, backward or to the side. Uke's reaction is normally to resist in the opposite direction to which he is being pushed or pulled, often coming off balance in the process. Tori then switches to a second technique, normally in the direction of Uke's movement.

Time phase combination

This tactic requires a strong attack, or multiple attacks, of a particular waza. If Uke's reaction is to change his posture or grip in order to nullify expectations of the same, or similar, attack, Tori can then launch a sudden attack of a totally different waza. By doing this, he is able to take advantage of the now weaker posture that Uke has developed in defending against the same waza for a long time.

Renzoku waza

Renzoku waza are standing techniques used in combination, where the second technique is a continuation of the first carried out in the same or a similar direction. Renzoku waza work on the basis that Tori is really committed with the initial attack, but has been unsuccessful as a result of Uke's defense. Because Tori has concentrated all his efforts in that direction, the second technique has to be in the same direction. Alternatively, Tori may deliberately set out to fool his opponent with the initial technique with the intention of moving into the second move when Uke is caught off guard. Examples of Renzoku waza are as follows:

Harai goshi into soto makikomi	(pages 152 and 153)
Hiza guruma into harai goshi	(pages 154 and 155)
Ippon seoi nage into kata guruma	(pages 156 and 157)
Ippon seoi nage into uchi makikomi	(page 158)
Kosoto gari into tani otoshi	(page 159)
Ogoshi into uki goshi	(page 160)
Osoto gake into osoto gari	(page 161)
Osoto gari into nidan kosoto gari	(pages 162 and 163)
Ouchi gari into kosoto gake	(pages 164 and 165)
Ouchi gari into kouchi gari	(pages 166 and 167)
Seoi nage into seoi otoshi	(pages 168 and 169)
Tai otoshi into uchimata	(pages 170 and 171)

Harai goshi into soto makikomi (hip sweep into outside winding)

Tori adopts a low sleeve and high lapel grip. He steps across, blocking the back of Uke's thigh with his thigh and pulls Uke forward. Uke's reaction is to block with the hips. Tori then pushes his hips farther through, lets go of Uke's neck, and wraps his arm over the arm that he is already holding. Tori rotates into the ground to complete the soto makikomi counter.

1. Shows the high collar and low sleeve grip.

2. Shows Tori's body placement and Uke's blocking action.

3. Shows Tori's grip change to a winding arm.

4. This shows the falling action and the required rotation of the body and arm to complete the technique.

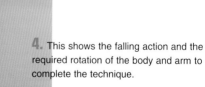

Hiza guruma into harai goshi (kneel wheel into hip sweep)

This is a body contact combination that requires the sole of Tori's foot to have contact with the front of Uke's knee. With a pull in a circular motion

1. Shows the high collar and low sleeve grip.

toward himself, Tori then swings the blocking leg behind him, transferring his weight. This enables him to step swiftly across and block the front of Uke's thigh, placing his hip in front of Uke's stomach. The change in direction of pull takes Uke off balance and then sweeps back Uke's legs.

2. Shows the foot placement of the hiza guruma action.

3. Shows the leg swing action and placement of the supporting foot.

4. Shows the placement of the blocking leg.

5. Shows the action of the blocking leg and the rotation required to complete the throw.

Ippon seoi nage into kata guruma (one-arm shoulder throw into shoulder wheel)

This is a body contact technique. Tori turns in for a one-arm shoulder throw using a two- or three-step entry. He pushes his hips too far through, so his shoulders are in contact with Uke's body. He then reaches through and hooks Uke's leg with his other hand, pulling Uke onto the top of his shoulder. He lifts Uke off the mat and rotates him onto his back.

1. Shows the single hand grip over Uke's arm onto the lapel.

2. Shows the body position required for the ippon seoi nage waza

3. Shows the change of back placement for the kata guruma.

4. Shows the lifting action and hand placement.

5. Shows the direction of the throw that completes this technique.

Ippon seoi nage into uchi makikomi
(one-arm shoulder throw into inner wheel)

The grip for this technique is normally on Uke's lapel. A three-step entry is used, whereby Tori takes her right foot forward, swinging the left foot behind. Removing the lapel grip, Tori traps Uke's arm in the inner elbow joint area. She then takes her right leg across, keeping it straight, and drives her hip into the ground in a winding motion.

1. Shows the single hand grip over Uke's arm onto the lapel.

2. Shows the body position for the ippon seoi nage.

3.

4. Shows the completion of uchi makikomi and the direction of the throw.

Kosoto gari into tani otoshi
(minor outer reap into valley drop)

1. Shows a low sleeve and mid-lapel grip.

2. Shows the lifting action of the kosoto gari.

3. The leg placement for the tani otoshi.

This is a body contact combination. Taking a middle lapel and low sleeve grip, Tori uses a one-step entry. Tori attacks with her right foot on the back of Uke's heel, convincing Uke she is trying to throw in that direction. Uke's reaction is to lift his foot out of the way. Tori immediately steps through and blocks the back of Uke's thighs and drops her body weight, pulling Uke backward down to the mat with tani otoshi.

4. Shows the direction of the throw to complete the technique.

Ogoshi into uki goshi
(major hip throw into floating hip throw)

This is a contact combination. Tori has his arm around Uke's waist using a three-step entry to achieve body contact with Uke. Uke attempts to escape by stepping around Tori's hips. When the outside of Uke's hips are level with Tori's hip, Tori pulls around the hip rather than over it, converting ogoshi into uki goshi.

1. Shows Tori's arm around Uke's waist and low sleeve grip.

2. Shows the ogoshi attack.

3. Shows Uke's block and avoidance, and Tori's hip placement for the uki goshi.

4. Shows the direction of the throw.

Osoto gake into osoto gari
(major outer hook into major outer reap)

1. Shows the high lapel and low sleeve grip.

2. Shows the osoto gake leg placement.

3. Shows the supporting leg placement.

This is a body contact combination. Using a one-step entry, it is important that Tori has a high lapel grip to enable her to control the head. She hooks the working leg behind the back of Uke. The initial contact point would be her heel into the back of Uke's supporting leg. Then Tori hops sideways (normally one to two hops), while simultaneously leaning forward. This action pushes Uke's balance onto his heels. Tori then sweeps the blocking leg through and up into the air.

4. Shows the completion of the osoto gari sweeping action.

Osoto gari into nidan kosoto gari (major outer reap into two-step minor outer reap)

This is a body contact combination. Tori uses a one-step entry. Tori must have a high grip on Uke's lapel, or over the shoulder, in order to have control of Uke's head. Tori steps behind Uke's leg, placing his foot on the ground.

1. Shows the high over-the-shoulder and low sleeve grip.

Uke's initial reaction is to swing around with her other leg, attempting to counter Tori. Tori immediately transfers his weight to his blocking leg and swings his free leg behind Uke's support leg.

2. Shows the osoto gari blocking leg action.

3. Shows the foot placement for the first stage of nidan kosoto.

4. Shows the nidan kisoto leg placement action.

5. Demonstrates the reaping action and head control in the completion of the throw.

Ouchi gari into kosoto gake
(major inner reap into minor outer hook)

1. Shows the low sleeve and mid-lapel grip.

This requires a three-step entry to the initial technique. Tori swings his leg behind and steps through with the right leg, achieving contact at the back of Uke's thigh, and the foot goes on the ground. Uke's reaction is to brace and block with her hips and then transfer her weight onto the rear of her legs and drive straight back.

2. Shows the leg placement for the ouchi gari action.

3. Demonstrates the placement of the hooking leg and the driving action.

Ouchi gari into kouchi gari (major inner reap into minor inner reap)

1. Shows the mid-lapel and low sleeve grip.

This is a feint combination. The initial entry for the ouchi gari consists of a two-step entry. Tori swings his leg behind him and places it on the mat. He drives the attacking leg forward, not intending to go as deep as he would if this was a direct attack. This action makes Uke move the attacked leg out of danger. Tori then promptly attacks with kouchi gari using the other leg, placing the sole of his foot on Uke's heel. Tori sweeps Uke's heel to his front, at the same time pushing with the hands to Uke's rear.

2. Shows the ouchi gari feint.

3. Shows Uke's step back from the ouchi gari attack.

4. Shows the placement of the foot for the kouchi gari.

5. Shows the completion of the throw, demonstrating the sweeping action of the leg.

Seoi nage into seoi otoshi
(shoulder throw into shoulder drop)

1 Morote seoi nage into seoi otoshi

1. Shows the mid-lapel and low sleeve grip.

2. Shows the morote seoi nage body and elbow position and Uke's blocking action.

3. Shows the seoi otoshi position.

4. Shows the direction of Uke's body that completes the throw.

This is a contact combination. This combination can be carried out using ippon seoi nage (see page 50) or morote seoi nage (see page 68). The initial grip can be a one-sleeve grip, throwing the other arm (inner elbow joint region) under Uke's armpit. Tori rotates his body with a three-step action until the back of his body is in contact with Uke's front. Uke's reaction is to block with her hips and front. Tori rotates the hips farther through and takes his right leg directly out. He can either put his knee on, or just off, the ground. This can also be done as a morote seoi nage, rather than ippon seoi nage into seoi otoshi. If morote seoi nage is used, the principle is the same except, instead of putting the inner elbow joint into Uke's armpit, Tori maintains the lapel grip and pushes the elbow across Uke's body.

2 Ippon seoi nage into seoi otoshi

1. Shows the ippon seoi nage body position.

2. Shows the change to the seoi otoshi body position.

3. Shows the direction Uke is thrown to complete this technique.

Tai otoshi into uchimata (body drop into inner thigh throw)

This is done with a three-step entry. Using a middle lapel and low sleeve grip, Uke blocks the third step (or is thrown by the initial tai otoshi attack). Uke's initial reaction is to block

1. Shows the middle lapel and low sleeve grip.

with his shin and then attempt to step over Tori's blocking leg. Tori then transfers his weight onto the opposite leg and hops backward, placing his hip in a straight line between Uke's legs, and lifts the sweeping leg up into the air, pulling it around.

2. Demonstrates the swinging leg entry to body contact.

3. Demonstrates the blocking leg for tai otoshi.

5. Tori's leg is between Uke's for the completion of the uchimata.

4. Demonstrates Uke's avoidance step.

Renraku waza (throws in the opposite direction)

Renraku waza are combinations of throwing techniques executed in rapid succession without a break. The second technique takes advantage of the reaction of an opponent and throws him or her in a completely different direction. These are throws in opposite directions, using the principle that any action by Tori will get a reaction from Uke. Examples of renraku waza that work in competition are as follows:

Ashi guruma into tani otoshi (leg wheel into valley drop)

1. Shows the middle lapel and low sleeve grip.

2. Demonstrates the half-step across entry for the ashi guruma.

3. Shows Uke's reaction and Tori's leg placement.

4. Show Tori's body position at the completion of the throw.

This is a feint attack. A one-step entry is used for the first attack, but Tori's body positioning should now be off center, to the left side of Uke. The attacking leg appears because of the rapid movement, as if it is going straight across in front of Uke's hips and legs. This feint is the ashi guruma element of the combination. Uke reacts strongly by bending his knees and possibly intending to block with his hips. Tori switches behind into a blocking position and drops down, pulling Uke with him. The second technique can also be substituted with kosoto gari (see page 60), where the blocking leg/foot becomes the sweeping leg/foot.

Deashi barai into tomoe nage (advancing foot sweep into circular throw)

1. Shows the middle lapel and low sleeve grip.

2. Shows Tori's deashi barai attack.

3. Shows Uke's step-back reaction.

4. Shows Tori's follow-up tomoe nage foot position.

This is normally a one-step action. Tori touches the advanced foot with the sole of his front foot, which, to be effective, Uke must believe to be a side-sweep attack. Uke steps back and, simultaneously, Tori pulls forward and places the sweeping leg onto Uke's stomach. Tori drops onto his back, taking Uke over in a full circle.

5. Shows the throwing position of Tori's body.

6. Demonstrates the circular action of tomoe nage at the completion of this throw.

Harai goshi into osoto gake (hip sweep into major outer hook)

1. Shows the high collar and low sleeve grip.

2. Demonstrates the harai goshi attack.

3. Demonstrates the change of direction into the osoto gake movement.

This is a body contact technique, which requires an initial three-step entry into the harai goshi. A high lapel grip is also needed. It is important that a high lapel grip is achieved on the third step to ensure good control of the head. Tori's sweeping leg is in position across the front of Uke's right thigh. Uke's reaction is to block with his hips and bend the knees. Tori maintains a strong positioning of the attacking leg. She hops on the supporting leg to Uke's side and drives the leg down into the gake (hooking) action. This technique can also turn into osoto gari (see page 80) with a sweeping action rather than a hook.

4. Shows the full throwing action of osoto gake at the completion of the technique.

Hiza guruma into osoto gari (knee wheel into major outer reap)

1. Shows the high collar and low sleeve grip.

2. Shows the foot placement on Uke's knee, making the hiza guruma feint.

3. Demonstrates the osoto gari position.

This is a feint attack. It is important with this throw to have a high lapel grip to control the head. With a two-step attack Tori steps toward Uke's side, simultaneously placing the sole of his foot level with Uke's knee (a degree of contact sometimes occurs). Uke's reaction is to resist in the opposite direction, normally by bending both knees. Tori switches, moving the leg placed on Uke's knee behind Uke's other leg and sweeps.

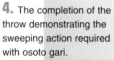

4. The completion of the throw demonstrating the sweeping action required with osoto gari.

Ippon seoi nage into kouchi gake
(one-arm shoulder throw into minor inner hook)

1. Grip

2. Feint

3. Body position

The aim of the initial technique is to achieve body contact, using the one-arm shoulder throw

4. Throw

technique, which requires Tori to grip on either the sleeve or the lapel. (This tends to be more successful on the the lower sleeve grip, although the lapel has a higher surprise element.) Tori initially takes a two-step entry inside Uke's leg, in a lunging action, but rotates his head and shoulders toward Uke's front. Tori's back is in contact with Uke's chest and the inner part of his elbow joint is underneath Uke's armpit. This convinces Uke that ippon seoi nage is about to take place. Tori's inside leg hooks onto Uke's leg and Tori drives back off his back leg, the supporting leg. This action is done as Uke defends and pushes his hips forward and leans backward, making himself more susceptible to the rear attack.

Kouchi gari into ippon seoi nage (minor inner reap into one-arm shoulder throw)

This technique requires a feint to catch Uke off guard. Using a one-step entry for the initial kouchi gari attack, with a one-handed lapel grip (alternatively, the grip can be on the sleeve) Tori places the initial attacking leg (foot) behind Uke's right leg. Uke's reaction is to take the leg away. Tori immediately swings round, placing her feet shoulder-width apart. Tori's back is against Uke's front. Tori bends her knees, pulling Uke forward over his center of gravity and rotates.

1. Shows the middle lapel and low sleeve grip.

2. Shows the kouchi gari action.

3. Demonstrates Uke's step-back reaction and Tori's placement of her arms.

4. The ippon seoi nage body position.

5. The completion of ippon seoi nage.

Kouchi gari into tai otoshi (minor inner reap into body drop)

1. Shows the middle lapel and low sleeve grip.

2. Demonstrates the kouchi gari feint.

3. Shows Uke's step-back reaction and Tori's body positioning entry.

4. Shows Tori achieving the body positioning for the tai otoshi throw.

This is a feint attack, which uses a one-step entry to the rear of Uke's heel. Tori places the sole of her foot on the ground. Uke's reaction is to step backward. Tori puts her weight on the attacking leg and rotates her other leg in a semicircle so that she is in a square-on position. Tori puts her weight on the circling leg and then transfers her weight to the front of Uke's shin, drawing Uke over the outstretched leg.

5. The completion of the technique showing the hand control and direction of the throw.

Osoto gake into seoi otoshi
(major outer hook into shoulder drop)

This is a body contact combination using a two-step entry. Tori steps forward with his support leg so he is sideways to Uke in order to execute the osoto gake. Tori then hooks the heel of the attacking leg behind Uke's knee. Uke's reaction is to resist to his front, as his expectation is of a rear action. Tori then repositions his attacking leg by sliding his hip through to the ground and re-establishing the hip below Uke's waist. At the same time, Tori pushes his elbow across under Uke's armpit while maintaining the lapel grip. The lifting of the leg comes from the straightening of Tori's knee.

1. Shows the middle lapel and low sleeve grip.

2. Shows the osoto gake body positioning.

3. Shows the marote seoi otoshi position.

4. Shows the completion of the seoi otoshi and the direction of the throw.

Ouchi gari into sasae tsurikomi ashi
(major inner reap into propping drawing ankle)

This is a body contact technique with a two-step entry. For the initial ouchi gari entry aspect of the combination, the attacking leg goes between Uke's legs, making contact with the lower calf. The attacking leg becomes the weight-bearing leg. Uke reacts by stepping backward. Tori's other leg then comes to the front of Uke's inner ankle, and the low sleeve grip and lapel grip are used to pull Uke toward Tori. Tori throws Uke over the blocking foot.

1. Shows the middle lapel and low sleeve grip.

2. Demonstrates the ouchi gari attack.

3. Shows Uke's step-back reaction and Tori's blocking foot placement for sasae tsurikomi ashi.

4. Shows the completion of sasae tsurikomi ashi and the direction in which Uke is thrown.

Osoto gari into yoko wakari (major outer reap into side separation)

With a two-step action Tori's support leg steps forward to a sideways stance to Uke. She drives the attacking leg back to the rear of Uke's leg for the initial osoto gari attack. Uke's reaction is to lean forward. Just prior to this, Tori lets go of the lapel grip and slides her arm underneath Uke's arm. It is also possible to maintain the lapel grip and slide the elbow under. Then Tori throws herself backward and just before she makes contact with the mat, rapidly spins her body, pulling Uke over.

1. Shows the middle lapel and low sleeve grip.

2. Demonstrates the osoto gari position.

3. Shows the hand placement and the falling action of the yoko wakari.

4. Demonstrates the rotation required to complete the yoko wakari technique.

Sasae tsurikomi ashi into deashi barai (propping drawing ankle into advancing foot sweep)

Tori takes a one-step entry, placing his attacking foot against the front of Uke's shin. Tori pulls Uke toward himself. Uke's reaction is to bend his knee and step over the blocking foot, immediately placing the avoiding foot on the ground over Tori's blocking foot. This action transfers weight onto the avoiding leg. Tori's original blocking foot becomes the support foot, as he lifts the other foot, turns the sole onto Uke's other foot, which now has less weight on it, and sweeps sideways. The hand action on the judogi is a circular motion, like turning a steering wheel.

1. Shows a mid-lapel and low sleeve grip.

2. Demonstrates the sasae tsurikomi ashi action.

3. Shows Uke's avoidance.

4. Demonstrates the deashi barai follow-up technique.

5. Shows the completion of the technique, demonstrating the full sweeping action of Tori's foot and leg.

Uchimata into kouchi gari (inner thigh throw into minor inner reap)

1. Shows the middle lapel and low sleeve grip.

2. Demonstrates the first step toward Uke.

3. Shows the second step of the supporting leg.

4. Demonstrates the uchimata action and Uke's block.

This is a body contact throw. With a two-step entry into the uchimata, Tori initially places the attacking leg through Uke's legs. The support leg takes up position between Uke's legs, achieving contact with the side of his body. Uke's reaction is to resist to his rear. Tori hops out, and on the way she uses the sole of her foot to connect with Uke's right heel, making a sweeping action. Coinciding with the sweep, Tori also pushes with both arms to Uke's rear. This combination works with either a high lapel grip or a middle lapel grip.

5. Demonstrates the kouchi gari foot placement required.

6. Shows the completion of the throw, demonstrating the full sweeping action of kouchi gari.

Kaeshi waza

These are countering techniques. If you are attacked, you must take action, whether it be to block the technique, move out of the way, or, preferably, to convert it to your advantage. If you do nothing, you will be thrown! A judoka should practice counter-throws so that they become second nature. As soon as an opponent comes in for a technique, it should be anticipated and countered. However, if a competitor merely waits for an opponent to attack so that he or she can counter, the competitor may receive a penalty for passivity. Kaeshi waza are counter-techniques within judo. For every technique with which you are attacked, there is a possible counter.

A counter is invariably a tactic where Uke positions his body and gripping pattern, thereby setting a trap for Tori, hoping Tori will attack, so that Uke can win with a counterattack, becoming the Tori. Although an attacking judoka is normally referred to as "Tori" and the judoka being thrown is referred to as "Uke," in this section of the book, "Tori" is used to indicate the judoka who makes the counter and actually throws. "Uke" refers to the judoka being countered, despite his original attack.

Ashi guruma countered by te guruma (leg wheel countered by hand wheel)

Uke attacks with ashi guruma, his front leg coming across Tori's thighs. Tori lets go of his sleeve grip, lowering down to take the inside of the thigh of Tori's attacking leg. Tori maintains the lapel grip. He then bends his knees, simultaneously pulling Uke onto him, and lifts. At the peak of the lift, Tori pulls the lapel toward him. This rotates Uke to a position flat on his back. This is also a useful counter against a harai goshi attack (see page 42).

1. Tori takes a mid-lapel and low sleeve grip.

3. Shows Tori's block and hand placement.

2. Demonstrates Uke's ashi guruma attack.

4. Shows Tori's lifting action.

5. Shows the direction required for the completion of the te gurma.

Deashi barai countered by kouchi gari (advancing foot sweep countered by minor inner reap)

Uke advances his foot, setting a trap. Tori sweeps with the sole of his foot, placing the sole of her foot on Uke's heel, and carries out a kouchi gari sweeping action.

1. Shows the middle lapel and low sleeve grip and Tori's foot slightly advanced.

2. Shows Uke's deashi barai attack.

3. Shows the foot placement for Tori's kouchi gari counter.

4. Demonstrates the sweeping action of kouchi gari at the completion of the throw.

Harai goshi countered by ura nage (hip sweep countered by rear throw)

Uke attacks with a harai goshi movement. Tori bends his knees and pulls Uke onto him. Powering from the legs and thrusting the hips up and away, Tori starts to fall backward and pulls Uke over his left shoulder. On the way to the ground, Tori rotates his body toward Uke.

1. Shows the middle lapel and low sleeve grip.

2. Shows Uke attacking with harai goshi and Tori's arm placement around Uke's waist.

3. Demonstrates the lifting action required.

4. Demonstrates the direction of the ura nage and Tori's falling action at the completion of the throw.

Harai goshi countered by ushiro goshi (hip sweep countered by rear hip throw)

Uke attacks with harai goshi. Tori bends his knees, simultaneously wrapping his arm around Uke's waist and pulling Uke onto his hips. Lifting with the hips by straightening the knees, Tori lifts Uke's feet off the ground and Uke lands on her back.

1. Shows the middle lapel and high sleeve grip.

2. Shows Uke attacking with harai goshi and Tori's arm placement around Uke's waist.

3. Demonstrates the lifting action.

4. Shows the completion and direction of the ushiro goshi.

Hiza guruma countered by ouchi gari (knee wheel countered by major inner reap)

Uke attacks Tori by placing his foot on Tori's knee. Tori has a low sleeve grip, which means her hand is close to Uke's attacking leg. Tori lets go of the sleeve and grabs Uke's leg. She then places the other leg behind Uke's support leg and lifts and sweeps backward, taking Uke's remaining leg away.

1. Shows the middle lapel and low sleeve grip.

2. Shows Uke attacking with hiza guruma.

3. Shows Tori's hand placement to Uke's leg.

4. Demonstrates the ouchi gari leg placement.

5. Shows the sweeping action of the ouchi gari at the completion of the technique.

Kosoto gari countered by uchimata
(minor outer reap countered by inner thigh throw)

Tori advances his foot close to Uke's front foot. To make this work, Tori needs a high lapel grip. Uke attempts to hook Tori's front leg, but Tori simultaneously changes the direction of his farthest leg by hopping so his toes are facing forward. At the same time, Tori lifts his leg and lowers the head into an uchimata position, using his arms to pull Uke on and, in conjunction with the leg movement, completes the technique.

1. Shows a high collar and low sleeve grip.

2. Shows Uke attacking with kosoto movement.

3. Demonstrates Tori's uchimata body placement.

4. Demonstrates the lifting leg of uchimata waza at the completion of the throw.

Kouchi gari countered by harai tsurikomi ashi (minor inner reap countered by lift-pull foot sweep)

Tori puts his foot forward as a target and attempts to make it look as if this is a weight-bearing foot. Uke attempts to sweep the rear of Tori's ankle with kouchi gari. Tori lifts the attacked leg to the front of Uke's shin, pulls Uke forward and, following the initial block, uses his foot to sweep Uke's leg away with the harai tsurikomi ashi.

1. Shows the mid-lapel and low sleeve grip.

2. Shows Uke's kouchi gari attack.

3. Demonstrates Tori's foot placement for the harai tsurikomi ashi.

4. Shows the sweeping action of harai tsurikomi ashi at the completion of the throw.

Morote garai countered with tawara gaeshi

Uke attacks with a double leg grab, morote garai, with a one-step lunge. Tori places his arms around Uke's stomach area and takes Uke over the shoulder to his rear.

1. Shows attacking positions for both Tori and Uke.

2. Shows Uke attacking with morote garai.

3. Demonstrates Tori's arm placement around Uke's waist.

4. Shows the direction and lifting action at the completion of the throw.

Okuriashi barai countered by tsubame gaeshi (double foot sweep countered by swallow swoop counter)

Tori places his foot in front of Uke; it looks weight-bearing. Uke attempts to sweep sideways. Tori reacts by bending his knee, and the force of Uke's attack swings past Tori's legs. Tori then straightens his leg and sweeps the heel of Uke's attacking leg, continuing the initiated motion.

1. Shows the middle lapel and low sleeve grip.

2. Uke attacks with okuriashi barai.

3. Shows Tori's avoidance action.

4. Shows the foot placement on the execution of the tsubame gaeshi technique.

5. Demonstrates the full sweeping action required to complete this throw.

Osoto gari countered by osoto gaeshi (major outer reap counter)

Tori positions her front leg close to Uke's front leg, setting a trap for Uke's closest leg to attack Tori's front leg, by placing his leg behind Tori's. It is important that Uke has no control over Tori's head. Tori's free leg then swings around in a rear half circle and immediately becomes weight-bearing. The attacked leg then becomes the sweeping leg and completes the technique.

1. Shows the high collar and low sleeve grip.

2. Shows Uke's osoto gari attack.

3. Shows how Tori breaks Uke's balance with leg placement.

4. Demonstrates the lifting leg action required.

5. Demonstrates the full action of osoto gaeshi at the completion of the technique.

Ouchi gari countered by kosoto gari (major inner reap countered by minor outer reap)

1. Shows the middle collar and low sleeve grip.

2. Shows Tori's ouchi gari attack.

3. Demonstrates Tori's lifting leg and foot placement.

Uke attacks with an ouchi gari to the inside of Uke's leg. It is imperative that Tori controls the space between the two judokas. On the initial attack, Tori rotates his hips and body toward Uke, attacking Uke's attacking leg. It is important that the sleeve grip is maintained throughout.

4. Demonstrates the full sweeping action at the completion of the technique.

Tsurikomi goshi countered by utsuri goshi (lift-pull hip throw countered by hip transfer throw)

Uke turns in for the tsurikomi goshi and achieves body contact. As he starts the action, Tori wraps his arm around Uke's waist and lifts with the rear hip throw action. The throwing action creates a space between Uke's hip and Tori's hips. Tori then swings his hips through in front of Uke. On Uke's descent, the front of his hips makes contact with the rear of Tori's hips and he is pulled over.

1. Shows a low sleeve and an around-the-back grip.

2. Shows Uke attacking with tsurikomi goshi.

3. Demonstrates Tori's lifting action.

4. Shows Tori's hip placement.

5. Demonstrates the rotation required at the completion of the technique.

Uchimata countered by tai otoshi (inner thigh throw countered by body drop)

1. Shows Uke with a mid-lapel and low sleeve grip. Tori has an inside lapel grip.

2. Demonstrates Uke's uchimata attempt.

3. Shows Tori's sidestep action.

4. Shows Tori's body positioning for tai otoshi.

It is important that Tori has a middle lapel grip and low sleeve grip, enabling her to have chest space between herself and Uke. Tori positions herself so her feet are just slightly wider than shoulder-width apart. The majority of Tori's weight is on the other leg and her body is slightly bent. Uke launches in for uchimata against Tori's leg. Tori sidesteps by lifting the leg and pushing her hips forward. The momentum of Uke's lifting leg takes Uke off balance. Tori immediately steps in front of Uke with her calf muscle across the front of Uke's shin. Tori rotates her hands to complete the tai otoshi.

5. Demonstrates the direction of the throw and the hand control required at the completion of tai otoshi.

chapter 4

Newaza (ground techniques)

The object of judo is to score ippon (see page 23). This can be achieved by throwing one's opponent flat on the back with impetus. It can also be achieved on the ground, by gaining a submission or holding one's opponent on the back for twenty-five seconds (using an accepted method).

If an opponent is immobilized for twenty-five seconds ippon is awarded, and this immediately finishes the contest. Lesser scores are achieved for shorter periods of holding. For example, after ten seconds a koka is scored, after fifteen seconds a yuko is scored, and after twenty seconds a waza ari is scored.

A submission also finishes the contest immediately. This can be accomplished by an armlock, which may only be applied to the elbow joint, or a strangle or choke on the neck. Uke signifies submission to a technique by tapping either Tori or the tatame twice with his hand. The foot can be stamped in submission if Uke's arms are trapped and, as a last resort, Uke can call "matte" (submit). It should be stressed that the objective is to gain submission, not to harm one's opponent. Judo students are trained to submit before damage can occur.

The Japanese word *gatame* is found in the names of both hold-downs, such as hon kesa gatame, and armlocks, such as ashi gatame. It actually means "to tighten" and, interestingly enough, holds were not timed originally. Instead the aim was to gain a submission.

In newaza (ground techniques), Uke will often adopt a defensive posture. This could be flat on his front or on his hands, or more likely elbows, and knees (this will often be referred to as the "all fours" position). Much groundwork capitalizes on Uke's defensive posture. Turnovers have been developed from these positions to obtain holds, armlocks, and strangles. Some armlocks and strangles can be applied directly from these positions. Another common position is for Uke to have one or both legs trapped between Tori's legs. Uke will usually be in a kneeling position, otherwise "matte" is called and both parties stand up.

Osaekomi waza
(hold-downs)

Please be advised that the holds that follow are demonstrated, in most cases, purely as holds using a cooperative Uke lying on his back. Anyone who has partaken in randori or contest judo will know that it is simply not that easy to get one's opponent into this position. There are infinite ways to get an opponent into a hold-down and, where possible, suggestions have been made.

Hon kesa gatame (basic scarf hold)

Hon kesa gatame is quite a versatile hold-down. It can be used from a variety of throws, especially those using a high lapel grip. This is because very little adjustment is required and Uke lands in a holding position. There are many newaza turnovers that result in hon kesa gatame, which is what makes it such a popular and effective technique.

When learning hon kesa gatame, Tori begins by sitting next to Uke almost with her back to Uke, but slightly turned toward Uke's head. The arm nearest Uke's head (for a right-handed technique, this will be the right arm) is placed around Uke's neck (like a scarf) and grips the jacket around the lapel or shoulder region.

Uke's right arm is then placed under Tori's left armpit and is squeezed tightly to maintain control. Tori leans on Uke's upper body. Tori's legs are spread in a hurdle-type position, ensuring her back leg is not trapped by Uke, as this will break the hold-down. Tori's legs stabilize Uke and prevent Tori from being turned off Uke.

Kami shiho gatame (upper four quarters hold)

This hold, as its name suggests, controls Uke's upper body. Kneeling just above Uke's head, Tori slides his arms under both of Uke's shoulders and grips the belt. Tori achieves chest contact at the same time. If Tori pulls the belt toward himself, the hold is tightened. Uke's head is under Tori's armpit. Tori pushes his stomach and hips to the floor and spreads his legs out straight with the feet wide apart, using his toes to push off the mat and assist his control of Uke. This technique can also be applied with the knees bent up close to Uke. In a contest situation, Tori may find it necessary to vary the leg position to counter Uke's struggle to escape.

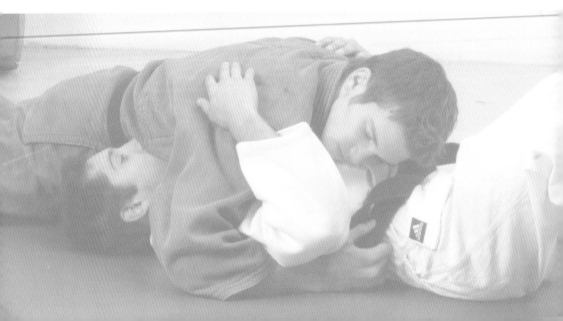

Kata gatame (shoulder hold)

This is normally used as a continuation from hon kesa gatame (see page 213), although it is a technique in its own right. If, from a hon kesa gatame position, Uke manages to release his right arm, he will push Tori's chest or neck in an attempt to escape. Tori utilizes Uke's struggle by pushing Uke's arm across his own face and placing her own neck or the side of her face against the tricep of Uke's arm. She then takes hold of the hand that is around Uke's neck and applies pressure. The legs can be in a hurdle position on the mat, as in hon kesa gatame, or can be strengthened by coming onto the nearest knee, with the other leg out straight and the foot pushing against the tatame for stability.

To prevent Uke from escaping, a helpful tip would be for Tori to release the grip with her left hand and pass her own lapel to the right hand. This secures the hold but also allows Tori to use her free (right) hand to maintain balance as Uke struggles.

Kuzure kami shiho gatame
(broken upper four-quarters hold)

This is any upper-body holding variation of the standard kami shiho gatame (see page 214). For example, from just above Uke's head, Tori slides her right arm under Uke's shoulder, gripping the belt as in kami shiho gatame. But she then places the left arm over Uke's arm and into the armpit region. She reaches back under Uke's arm to grip Uke's lapel; chest contact is achieved and the legs are spread to maintain balance. This is just one variation. There are others, such as placing the right arm over and the left arm under Uke's shoulders; or placing both arms over (with elbows in Uke's armpits); or turning Uke over using a double lapel grip and maintaining control with the lapels once Uke is on his back.

Kuzure kesa gatame (broken scarf hold)

Kuzure means "broken" and kuzure kesa gatame is therefore a variation of hon kesa gatame (see page 213). Tori begins by sitting next to Uke almost with her back to Uke, but slightly turned toward Uke's head. Instead of placing the arm nearest the head around Uke's neck, as with hon kesa gatame, Tori leans across Uke's chest and slides her right arm under Uke's left armpit and either holds the jacket near the lapel or places the palm of her

hand on the mat to stabilize herself. Tori's right arm, as with hon kesa gatame, is secured under Tori's left armpit.

Makura kesa gatame (pillow scarf hold)

Tori positions herself as if applying hon kesa gatame (see page 213). That is, Tori sits in close to Uke, with her right arm placed around Uke's neck. Instead of gripping the lapel or shoulder region, Tori grips her own thigh. In doing so, Uke's head is raised by Tori's forearm and immobilized. Uke's right arm is secured under Tori's left armpit and Tori's legs are spread in a hurdle position as in hon kesa gatame.

Mune gatame (chest hold)

This technique requires close chest-to-chest contact. From beside Uke, Tori reaches across Uke's body, trapping Uke's arm at the shoulder. Very often the head is also secured to increase the level of control over Uke. Tori would normally be on both knees, using them to apply close contact.

Sangaku gatame (triangular hold)

This is normally used as an escape move from a hold such as yoko shiho gatame (see page 222). The first move is to break Uke's hold by pushing his head down toward Tori's legs. Tori then puts his leg over Uke's head, trapping the side of Uke's head against Tori's thigh. The front of Tori's ankle goes to the back of Tori's opposite knee, applying pressure. This can sometimes result in the technique becoming sangaku jime (see page 235), a strangle. Tori,

while maintaining a strong grip with his legs, rolls on top of Uke to secure the hold. Tori can grip Uke's trouser leg to enhance stability.

Alternatively, this hold is used when Tori is attacking with sangaku jime but is unable to apply the strangle. In this case, while maintaining the grip with the legs, Tori hoists himself on top of Uke, usually using Uke's trouser leg as an anchor.

Tate shiho gatame (lengthwise four-quarters hold)

Initially Tori sits astride Uke's abdomen with his knees in contact with the mat. Tori hooks his heels at the back of Uke's legs with toes to the outside and traps either one or both of Uke's arms (generally one arm is trapped) across Uke's body. To secure the arm in place, Tori places his neck against Uke's arm. Uke's hand is forced around his own neck, and Tori inserts his right arm under Uke's neck and holds his other hand, applying pressure to maintain the hold. Tori can use his legs and left hand to stabilize himself as Uke tries to escape.

Ushiro kesa gatame (reverse scarf hold)

This technique normally occurs following a makikomi throw (see pages 40, 44, and 85). Tori lands facing Uke's legs: the arm and body have been rolled and Uke's arm is across Tori's back, with the wrist trapped under Tori's armpit.

The holding pressure comes from Tori maintaining the wrap movement; her other hand reaches over Uke's body and holds either the trouser leg, which she pushes down, or she can hold the belt.

Yoko shiho gatame (side four-quarters hold)

This hold requires close chest contact. Positioned on one side of Uke, Tori slides an arm under Uke's head: the hand grips either the lapel or shoulder region of the jacket. Tori's other arm reaches over Uke's nearest leg and under the far leg, preferably anchoring onto the belt. If the belt is out of reach, a similar result is possible by gripping the bottom of the skirt of the jacket. The position of Tori's chest should be as close to Uke's head as possible. A good 60 percent of Tori's upper body should be on top of

Uke. His stomach can be flat against the ground and the legs can be in various positions. For example, they can be flat to the mat and spread out, or the knees can be drawn up close to the body in a kneeling position.

Shime waza
(strangles/chokes)

The principle of a strangle or a choke is to apply pressure to the carotid artery located at either side of the neck—this cuts off or slows down the blood supply to the brain—or to put pressure on the windpipe, which shuts off the air supply to the lungs. In a contest, or randori, situation an initial strangle to the carotid artery may turn into a choking action of the windpipe or vice versa. Irrespective of the application, both achieve the same result in sport judo terms: they gain a submission (or referee's intervention) and an outright win. Referees are aware of the dangers of such a situation and can call ippon if they believe Uke may become unconscious.

Accuracy of the hand placement when executing a stranglehold is vital to the success of the technique. The legs very often assist in controlling an opponent. Safety is an important issue, as these techniques can cause dizziness, unconsciousness, and, potentially, death. All judoka are trained to signal submission before any damage occurs.

Within this section, reference will often be made to the "cutting edge" of the arm. This merely refers to the inner bony part of the forearm, which digs into the neck when applying a stranglehold.

Gyaku juji jime (reverse cross strangle)

Gyaku juji jime requires Tori to have the fingers of both hands inside the lapels of Uke's jacket. His arms should be crossed at the wrists, with the back of one wrist against the front of the other. His fingers should be deep enough into the jacket to enable the cutting edge of the wrist to touch the carotid artery area. If Tori pulls down and then pushes out, he pushes the muscles that protect the carotid artery to one side, and this should result in immediate submission (one to four seconds). If an immediate submission does not occur (up to ten seconds), this invariably means the wrist action is not accurately on the carotid artery. This strangle is usually applied when Tori is on his back and Uke is between his legs, or if Tori is sitting astride Uke, in a tate shiho gatame position (see page 220).

Gyaku juji jime, kata juji jime (see page 230) and nami juji jime (see page 232) are all very similar strangles and differ only in the way that the lapel is gripped.

Hadaka jime (naked strangle)

This is a neck choke. The reason that this is "naked" is because no element of the judogi is used. This means that there are many varieties of strangles that don't use the cloth of the judogi; they are all called hadaka jime. Two of them are described below.

Version 1:

This requires Tori to be behind Uke, sliding his arm around to the front of Uke's throat. The inside of the elbow should be level with the front-middle section of Uke's neck, and the arm bent. The cutting edge of Tori's forearm is level with one side of the carotid artery, while the bicep muscle targets the other. To apply pressure, Tori grasps the bicep of his own opposite arm and places that arm behind the back of Uke's head, pushing forward with his chest and squeezing his arms together.

Version 2:

This actually targets the windpipe area initially, rather than the carotid artery, although it can also apply pressure to the carotid artery, depending on the size and strength of Uke's neck and/or the amount of pressure applied. From behind Uke, Tori positions the cutting edge of his forearm against the front-middle section of Uke's throat. Tori then holds the hand of the strangle arm with his other hand and can either place his chest against the back of Uke's neck or shoulder. As with all strangles this is normally done in ground grappling (newaza). It can be applied when Uke is defending on his front, or in an all-fours position, or if Uke is rolled over, ending up between Tori's legs (with both Uke and Tori facing in the same direction).

Jigouku jime (hell strangle)

Uke is on all fours and Tori hooks her heel into Uke's inner elbow joint area using her other arm to grasp Uke's wrist under his armpit. Simultaneously, Tori slides her other hand, thumb first, under Uke's chin and places her wrist level with Uke's carotid artery. Tori then rolls sideways onto her back and applies pressure with her arms and leg. Uke's arms are immobilized by Tori's arm and leg, preventing him from defending against the strangle.

Jigouku jime (hell strangle)

This technique is normally attempted against Uke defending on the ground on all fours with weight on his elbows. Tori hooks his foot on the inside elbow on one of Uke's arms, keeping his weight on Uke's back. He slides one hand under Uke's chin, positioning the edge his strangling wrist against the cateriod. He hooks his other hand inside the other arm, then Tori falls onto his own back while controlling Uke's arms with the leg and arm grip. He applies pressure to the cateriod with his wrist in a circling action.

Kata ha jime (single lapel strangle)

This strangle is done from behind Uke, with Tori sliding the right hand under Uke's chin, thumb inside Uke's left lapel, and getting as close as possible to the carotid area. Tori places his left hand under Uke's armpit area, lifting Uke's arm, and places the back or front of the hand to the rear of Uke's neck. This ultimately stabilizes the head and Tori can, in fact, have a slight pushing action with the left hand while pulling with the right hand. Tori then brings Uke's lapel against the carotid artery. This technique is usually attempted when it has not been possible to place the cutting edge of the wrist accurately against the carotid area.

Kata juji jime (single cross strangle)

Kata juji jime is similar to both gyaku juji jime (see page 224) and nami juji jime (see page 232) and is applied when Tori and Uke are facing each other. With kata juji jime, one hand grips the lapel with the fingers in and the other with the thumb in. The arms are crossed at the wrists. The hands need to be deep inside the jacket, thus enabling the cutting edge of the wrist bone to be touching the carotid artery area. As with gyaku juji jime and nami juji jime, this strangle is usually applied when Tori is on his back and Uke is between his legs, or when Tori is sitting astride Uke in a tate shiho gatame position (see page 220). To apply the strangle if Tori is on his back, he pulls forward and draws the elbows apart. If Uke is on his back, Tori pushes the elbows apart and drives them down toward the mat. If an immediate submission is not achieved, this means the wrist action is not accurately on the carotid artery. Gyaku juji jime and nami juji jime are very similar strangles to kata juji jime and differ only in the way the lapel is gripped.

Koshi jime (hip strangle)

This strangle is attempted when Uke is on his front or in an all-fours position. The position requires one hand to be under Uke's chin with the thumb inside Uke's lapel. This places the cutting edge of Tori's wrist against Uke's carotid artery, and Tori's armpit on the back of Uke's neck. Tori swings his leg through and places his hip against Uke's side (the same side as the hand grip to the neck). Tori exerts pressure on Uke's neck, using his hip as the base.

Nami juji jime (standard cross strangle)

As with both gyaku juji jime (see page 224) and kata juji jime (see page 230), nami juji jime can be performed when Tori is on her back and Uke is between her legs, or when Tori is sitting astride Uke.

Tori slides both thumbs deep inside the lapel of Uke's jacket: the fingers latch onto the outside of the lapel, with palms facing down. Tori's arms are crossed at the wrists, making a triangle with the back of Uke's jacket. Tori's aim is to reduce the size of the triangle and to apply pressure to the sides of Uke's neck, targeting the carotid artery. The strangle is applied by executing a scissor-type movement with the arms as Tori pulls Uke forward if he is underneath her, or pushes down if Uke is on top.

Okuri eri jime (sliding lapel strangle)

This is a rear strangle, applied from behind an opponent. Tori sits on Uke's back, placing one arm around the front of Uke's neck and sliding the hand under his chin. The hand placement should be far enough around Uke's lapel to ensure that the cutting edge of Tori's wrist is against the carotid area of the neck. Her other hand comes under Uke's armpit and takes the opposite lapel to achieve stability: quite often Tori is on Uke's back in a piggy-back type position, maintaining control of Uke. Tori pulls the lapel grip at the neck in a semicircular motion, while pulling the lower lapel grip straight down. This applies pressure on the carotid artery.

Ryote jime (double-handed strangle)

This strangle is applied while facing Uke, and the hand placement needs to be accurate. This technique can be done in one of two ways. First, Tori places both of her thumbs inside Uke's lapel, with the fingers on the outside. The knuckles of the thumbs target the carotid arteries, pushing into the side of the neck. Alternatively, gripping as before, Tori rotates the finger knuckles with a screwing action against Uke's jacket and into the sides of Uke's neck. Tori pulls Uke's head down at the same time.

Sangaku jime (triangle strangle)

There are various methods of applying sangaku jime. When Uke is kneeling between Tori's legs, he will often try to escape by getting an arm free and will try to lift and turn Tori off. However, as Uke does so, Tori takes a strong grip of Uke's wrist and wraps his legs around Uke's head and trapped arm. Tori's right leg hooks behind his left knee, and, while still pulling on the wrist, Tori uses his left leg to push down, squeezing with the thighs. This closes the space around Uke's neck and should, if applied correctly, result in a submission.

Sangaku jime can also be implemented when Uke is in an all-fours position. One of the many examples from this position starts with Tori in front of Uke's head, sliding his knee in between Uke's head and shoulder, keeping it as close to the head as possible. Tori forces the heel of the other leg tightly behind Uke's elbow. Tori draws his knee and heel together, and then, using Uke's arm, he rolls him over onto his back (Tori will be on his side). Tori secures Uke's free arm with the belt or cloth from his jacket and reaches over and pulls Uke's trapped arm toward himself (an armlock can be applied from here, see pages 238–243). Tori adjusts his legs, if necessary, and completes the strangle by ensuring the right foot is under the left calf and by bringing the left leg toward himself while squeezing his thighs.

Sode guruma jime
(sleeve wheel strangle)

This is a rear strangle, performed when Uke is on his front. Tori takes one hand over Uke's shoulder to his farthest lapel. Tori crosses his other arm to the top of Uke's judogi sleeve, which means Tori's arms are now crossed at the back of Uke's neck and applying pressure there.

Tsurikomi jime (thrusting strangle)

This strangle is applied while facing Uke. It can be executed standing but is normally successful with Uke on his back. Tori has a double lapel grip—one hand with the fingers inside the lapel and the other hand with the thumb inside the lapel. Tori uses the grip with the thumb to pull Uke's lapel straight down. With the other grip, he uses the fingers to push the jacket across and aim for the carotid area of the neck.

Kansetsu waza (armlocks)

In judo, as with a strangle, an armlock is normally used in ground techniques (newaza). The objective is to apply pressure on the elbow joint. In sport judo, armlocks to joints other than the elbow joint are forbidden. It is also prohibited to throw someone being held with an armlock: the element of control is removed and Uke is highly susceptible to injury.

It is often difficult to tell where the elbow joint is under an opponent's judogi. A helpful tip when applying an armlock that involves straightening the arm is to pull in the direction of the little finger. That is, if the little finger is down (and the thumb up), take the arm down. Bear in mind, also, that you may have to make slight adjustments to counteract the independent wrist movement.

Ashi gatame (leg armlock)

This technique is applied when Uke is between Tori's legs. If Uke takes a lapel grip on Tori's jacket, Tori maneuvers onto his own hip, simultaneously pulling Uke's arm and following his leg over the arm, placing the foot under Uke's chin.

Hara gatame (stomach armlock)

This technique is usually attempted when Uke is in a defensive posture, on her hands and knees. Tori hooks his heel to the inside of Uke's elbow, drawing the arm out with the heel to straighten it. At the same time, he pushes his stomach into Uke's shoulder. Invariably Uke will collapse onto her front. Tori then crosses the hooking leg over to his other leg, still maintaining pressure on Uke's shoulder with his stomach.

Hiza gatame (knee armlock)

This armlock is applied when Uke is between Tori's legs and is using a lapel grip to push her hands into Tori's chest. Tori grabs Uke's wrist and maneuvers onto his farthest hip, simultaneously pulling the arm straight. This can be very fast and effective if, as Tori turns onto his side, he uses his foot to push Uke's knee back, causing Uke to collapse. Tori then places his knee on Uke's elbow area, exerting pressure with his leg and arm to apply the armlock.

Juji gatame (cross armlock)

This is usually applied with Uke on her back, although it can be done in an upside-down position. There are many entries for juji gatame, ranging from turnovers to the extravagant transfer from tomoe nage (see page 114) into juji gatame. The cross element of this technique refers to Tori's legs, which are placed across Uke's body. This positioning gives Tori a good degree of control over Uke. With Uke on her back, Tori anchors onto Uke's arm. With his legs on either side of Uke's arm, Tori holds the arm secure with his thighs. Applying pressure to the joint, Tori uses his body weight to control a resisting Uke. He extends the arm, holding both hands on Uke's wrist, and uses the groin area as a fulcrum. This applies pressure on Uke's elbow joint. If necessary, Tori raises his hips to increase the leverage on the arm.

Kesa garame
(scarf hold lock)

Tori has Uke in a kesa gatame hold-down (see page 213). Tori may lose grip of the arm under his armpit, or will intentionally release the grip in an attempt to bring the contest to an early finish. He then takes hold of Uke's right arm at the wrist and uses his thigh as a fulcrum, pushing Uke's arm down over his leg. If this does not create sufficient pressure, Tori can use his left knee to increase the pressure on the arm (a variation of hiza gatame, see page 240).

Ude garami (entangled armlock)

This entangled armlock is most successful when Uke is on her back. Tori lays across Uke, using his body weight to establish an element of control. Tori attacks Uke's arm by reaching across and grasping her wrist. Tori's other hand goes under the tricep area of Uke's arm and grasps his own wrist, thus making a figure-four shape. He then pulls the arm into Uke's side, pushes his own wrist down and in toward Uke's body and lifts his own forearm to apply pressure to the elbow joint.

Ude gatame (armlock)

Ude gatame is a straight armlock. It is most successful when Uke is on her back and attempting to push Tori off. Using this arm to his own advantage, Tori places both hands on Uke's elbow and pushes with his chest while pulling with both hands.

Waki gatame
(armpit armlock)

With Uke defending on her front, Tori gains control of Uke's body by lying across her back with the upper part of his body. Tori grips Uke's wrist and pulls the arm out straight, placing his upper arm at Uke's shoulder, and exerting pressure with the wrist grip.

chapter 5

Newaza (combination and counter-techniques)

As with standing work (tachi waza, see pages 148–209), combinations and counters can also be used in the groundwork element of judo. There is a huge variety of moves, as judoka are constantly developing new ways to manipulate opponents in order to get them into a hold or gain a submission.

Renzoku waza/renraku waza

Combinations in newaza (ground techniques) normally involve Tori achieving a hold or armlock while endeavoring to score the ippon, but starting to lose control during the course of the struggle. Tori has two choices in this situation: he can try to maintain control either by using the original technique again, or by switching to another groundwork technique. Some examples of newaza combinations are shown below:

Kesa gatame into kata gatame	(page 246)
Kesa gatame into hiza gatame	(page 247)
Kuzure kesa gatame into ude garame	(page 248)
Kuzure kami shiho gatame into ushiro kesa gatame	(page 249)
Yoko shiho gatame into juji gatame	(page 250)

Kesa gatame (scarf hold)
into kata gatame (shoulder hold)

Tori has applied kesa gatame, but during the struggle Uke manages to free the arm being held across Tori's chest and under Tori's armpit. Tori has a choice of trying to regain the arm, or of pushing the elbow across Uke's face and locking his neck into Uke's tricep muscle to strengthen the hold. Tori then grasps his own hands.

1. Shows the head control, arm control, and leg position of kesa gatame.

2. Shows Uke's arm escape and Tori's push on Uke's elbow.

3. Shows the elbow trapped against Uke's head.

Kesa gatame (scarf hold)
into hiza gatame (knee armlock)

Uke is being held with kesa gatame. During the course of the struggle, Uke manages to free the arm that was being held across Tori's chest and under Tori's armpit. Tori positions his knee under Uke's elbow joint, and grabs the inside of Uke's wrist, applying pressure to the elbow joint using the knee as a fulcrum.

1. Shows how Uke's arm escapes from the kesa gatame hold.

2. Shows the armlock being applied by Tori's knee.

Kuzure Kesa gatame (broken scarf hold) into ude garame (entangled armlock)

Uke is being held with kesa gatame. She has tried rolling Tori off, but Tori has countered with kuzare kesa gatame, taking his arm under Uke's armpit. Uke uses her arm in an attempt to push Tori off. Tori releases the controlling arm and reaches across to Uke's wrist. Tori's hand, which was under Uke's armpit, grabs Tori's own wrist and applies ude garame.

1. Demonstrates kuzure kesa gatame.

2. Shows Uke's attempt to escape.

3. Shows the initial grip pattern required for ude garame.

4. Shows the application of ude garame.

Kuzure kami shiho gatame (broken upper four-quarters hold) into ushiro kesa gatame (reverse scarf hold)

Uke is being pinned in the kami shiho gatame position. During the course of the struggle, Tori adapts to this, adjusting his under-the-shoulder grip to under the inside of Uke's arm. Tori then swings the nearest leg to Uke's head under Uke's shoulder, maintaining his grip of Uke's head.

1. Demonstrates kuzure kami shiho gatame.

2. Shows the step pattern required to the ushiro kesa gatame position.

3. Demonstrates ushiro kesa gatame.

Yoko shiho gatame (side four-quarters hold) into juji gatame (cross armlock)

Tori is holding Uke with yoko shiho gatame, which requires good chest contact. Uke attempts to escape by pushing away from Tori and placing his hand on the chest, attempting to create space. As Uke's push develops, Tori releases the grip and sits up suddenly, grasping Uke's nearest wrist. He swings one or two legs over Uke's body and/or face, levering back into juji gatame. This technique can also work using the same principle from tate shiho gatame (see page 230).

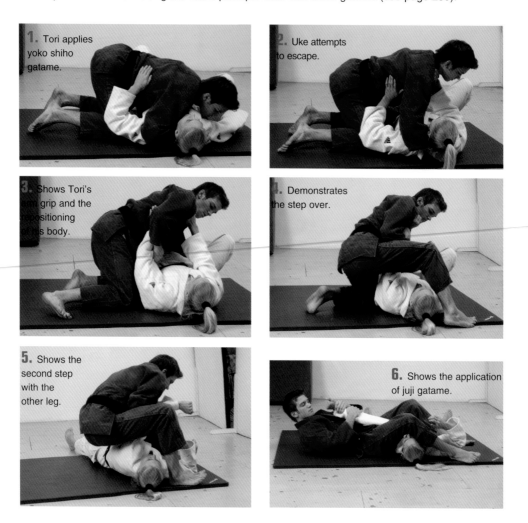

1. Tori applies yoko shiho gatame.

2. Uke attempts to escape.

3. Shows Tori's arm grip and the repositioning of his body.

4. Demonstrates the step over.

5. Shows the second step with the other leg.

6. Shows the application of juji gatame.

Kaeshi waza

Kaeshi waza are techniques that overcome an opponent's attack and in which the opponent is countered. As with standing techniques, it is also possible to make counter-techniques in groundwork. Although the initial reaction is to either defend or escape, it is possible to set traps and/or create chances to counter an opponent's techniques. As with the tachi waza counters (see pages 148–209), to save confusion in this section, "Tori" is used to indicate the judoka who will be making the counter to become the dominant party. "Uke" refers to the judoka being countered, despite his original attack.

kata juji jime (single cross strangle) countered by ashi gatame (leg armlock)

In groundwork, an opponent will attempt to apply this technique while facing Tori. Starting with Tori on his back and Uke in a chest-to-chest position, this strangle initially requires Uke's arm to become straight. Tori grabs one of the wrists, does not try to break the strangle, but maneuvers himself onto his hip. At the same time, he takes the leg over Uke's arm. His ankle goes under Uke's chin, applying pressure to the arm—this is ashi gatame.

1. Uke attempting front strangle.

2. Shows Tori positioning his body.

3. Demonstrates the application of ashi gatame.

Yoko shiho gatame (side four-quarters hold) countered by kata te kata ashi jime (one-hand-one-leg strangle)

Tori is being held with yoko shiho gatame. During the course of the struggle, he slips his hand under Uke's chin and grasps the farthest lapel, trying to get as deep as possible in order to get close to the carotid artery. Tori then lifts his leg as high as he can past Uke's leg and brings the back of the knee in contact with the side of Uke's neck. The thigh is in contact with the carotid area. Tori applies pressure with his hand and leg simultaneously to apply the strangle.

1. Uke holds Tori with yoko shiho gatame.

2. Shows Tori's placement of hands for the strangle.

3. Demonstrates Tori applying kata ashi jime.

Yoko shiho gatame (side four-quarters) countered by sangaku jime (triangle strangle)

Tori is being held with yoko shiho gatame. He grips the back of Uke's lapel with a thumb grip and uses the forearm to push against Uke's neck. At the same time he swings his leg up and, positioning the back of it against Uke's neck, he pushes down. Tori then places the back of the knee on the front of the upper part of the foot. The position of the legs means that Uke's head is trapped, as is one of Uke's arms. The squeezing action applies pressure to the carotid artery, ultimately achieving a submission.

1. Uke holds Tori with yoko shiho gatame.

2. Shows Tori pushing Uke's head.

3. Demonstrates the first stage of the strangle.

4. Tori applies sangaku jime.

index

bibliography and credits

Bibliography

Aida: **Kodokan Judo**
pub. W. Foulsham and Co. Ltd (1990)

Inokuma & Sato, BJ: **Best Judo**,
pub. Kodansha (1979)

Kashiwazki, K.: **Fighting Judo**,
pub. Pelham Books (1985)

Kawashi, M: **Katas of Judo**,
Pub. W. Foulsham & Company Limited (1954)

Kwashi & Welsh, AR: **Judo**,
pub. Putnam & Company Limited (1949)

Kawamura, T & Baigo, T: **Kodokan Dictionary of Judo**,
pub. The Foundation of The Kodokan Judo Institute (2000)

About the author

Roy Inman, OBE, judo 8th dan

Former international judo champion

Coach at 4 Olympic Games

Coach at 18 World Judo Championships

Senior instructor at the London Budokwai Martial Arts Club

Currently high performance coach at Bath University

Acknowledgements

I would like to extend my sincere thanks to Michelle Holt, a member of the British Judo Team, for her combat skills and help in the production of this book, and without whom it may never have happened. I would also like to thank Jason Parsons and Tom Reed, members of the British Judo Team for their photogenic qualities. Last, but not least, my wife, Carol, for her constant support and patience.